**Post-Communist
Reform**

Post-Communist Reform

Pain and Progress

Olivier Blanchard
Maxim Boycko
Marek Dabrowski
Rudiger Dornbusch
Richard Layard
Andrei Shleifer

The MIT Press
Cambridge, Massachusetts
London, England

United Nations University/World Institute for Development Economics
Research (UNU/WIDER)
Helsinki, Finland

This book was set in Palatino by .eps Electronic Publishing Services and
was printed and bound in the United States of America.

Library of Congress Cataloging-in-Publication Data

Post-communist reform : pain and progress / Olivier Blanchard . . . [et
al.]
  p. cm.
Includes bibliographical references and index.
ISBN 0-262-02362-8
  1. Russia (Federation)—Economic conditions—1991- 2. Former Soviet
republics—Economic conditions. 3. Europe, Eastern—Economic conditions—1989- I. Blanchard, Olivier (Olivier J.)
HC340.12.P67 1993   93-1732
338.947—dc20   CIP

Contents

Foreword

The World Economy Group is an independent group of leading economists set up by WIDER to report on major economic issues. In 1991, they produced a widely acclaimed report on the general issues of economic transition entitled *Reform in Eastern Europe*. The process of reform was still young. It is now three years old, and much has been learned during those three years. It is time to return and assess the evidence. This is what they offer in this report.

For this purpose, the group has been widened this year to include three additional members who have all been heavily involved in the reform process. Two of them, Maxim Boycko, Director of the Russian Privatization Center, and Andrei Shleifer, Professor of Economics at Harvard University, have been among the architects of the Russian privatization program. The third, Marek Dabrowski, is Chairman of the Polish Council of Ownership Changes and former Deputy Minister of Finance in the first Polish reform government. One of the members of the group, Paul Krugman, could not participate this year.

In their first report, the authors identified three main steps of the reform process, macrostabilization and price liberalization, privatization, and restructuring. They return to those three themes in this report. As could be expected, their report is neither dogmatic nor bland. They take up the issue of whether Russia's reform without stabilization can succeed or is a pact with the devil, bound to end in failure. They argue that the way to make progress in privatization is to realize that privatization is not about distribution or sale of the assets of "the state," but rather of assets with many claimants: workers, managers, local authorities, ministries, all with an incentive to oppose a dilution of their claims. Recognizing that convertibility is unlikely to be quickly implemented in the republics of the ex–Soviet Union, they draw on the experience of the post–World War II European Payments Union to recommend a similar payments system. Examining the progress of restructuring in Poland, they show the damage from the lack of progress on privatization on the evolution of state firms, and they look behind the impressive private sector growth numbers to point out its inability to replace state firms any time soon.

This only gives a glimpse of the many arguments of this report. I warmly recommend a full reading to all those concerned with the difficult problems of economic transition.

Lal Jayawardena
Director of WIDER
Helsinki
January 31, 1993

1   Overview

Two years ago, this group produced a report on the general issues of economic transition entitled *Reform in Eastern Europe*. Reform was just starting. As we were writing, Polish stabilization was not yet six months old. Privatization programs were still just programs. And restructuring was an issue left for the future. Analysis and advice had to be based on the accumulated wisdom of experience from other countries and other times; how relevant all that was for Eastern Europe was hotly debated.

Two years later, much has happened and much has been learned. The reform process is very much alive. For many Central European countries, stabilization is now a thing of the past, although inflation is still high and the risk of accelerating inflation always present. Privatization plans have been implemented, although progress has been painfully slow. Restructuring is at the top of the agenda, and governments struggle with how best to help growth, how fast to close unprofitable state firms, and so on. And surely one of the most important events of 1992 is the start of

---

Written by Olivier Blanchard and Richard Layard.

economic reform in Russia. Under the force of political realities, Russia is following a different route. Stabilization has not been attempted, money creation and inflation are running high. But many prices now clear markets, and privatization is proceeding at a fast pace.

In this new report, we thus return to the three steps of reform we had identified earlier, stabilization and price liberalization, privatization, and restructuring. We assess progress, mistakes, and issues for the future.

Stabilization and Price Liberalization

The prevailing wisdom in 1991, and one embodied in our report of that year, was that both stabilization and price liberalization were preconditions for a successful reform process. The arguments were political, macroeconomic, and microeconomic. The political argument was that the government had to send a clear signal that it was going to balance the budget, and that it was no longer committed to extending unlimited credit to loss-making firms. The macroeconomic argument was that, lacking stabilization, inflation would turn to hyperinflation, with its attendant large dislocations. The microeconomic argument was that, for privatization and restructuring to proceed in the right direction, prices had to be right, and firms could not avoid market discipline.

This was the thinking behind the Central European stabilizations. Russia, however, has not followed this route. Most

prices were liberalized in January 1992. But macrostabilization was never implemented, so that during 1992 inflation
never fell below 9 percent a month. This raises two issues.
Why has there been no stabilization? And can reform succeed nevertheless? These are the issues we explore in
chapter 2.

The first question is easier to answer than the second. Going
beyond the conflicts between the Central Bank and the
government, the basic answer is that stabilization was not
implemented because there was insufficient support for the
unemployment that would have resulted. In April 1992, the
People's Congress told the government that the top priority
was to "stabilize production." Concretely, this meant prop-
ping up employment in state firms through credit and thus
money creation. Whether or not this message reflected the
priorities of people at large, the message was clear that, for
the time being, no government could stabilize and survive.
The reformers in the government thus had a choice. Their
main purpose was to turn Russia into a capitalist economy.
To do this, they needed to retain power, and to retain power,
they had to accept a massive growth of credit to state firms.
By this strategy, they secured a major triumph on another
front. In June, the Supreme Soviet approved a plan for the
fastest privatization in history, and at the time of this writing, the plan is being implemented.

The second question is much harder to answer. Was prevailing wisdom right, and is the trade of no-stabilization for
privatization a pact with the devil? One can see many ways
the current course can go wrong, and, at the time of this

writing, events provide little reassurance. Maintaining employment in existing firms does not allow for the release of people and factors needed elsewhere. But one can think of worse and more immediate consequences. First, there is no such thing as steady high inflation. Indeed, generous credit and low unemployment are both fueling accelerating wage demands and, at the time of writing, high inflation appears to have become hyperinflation. Hyperinflations never last very long. Second, the political signals given by the lack of control of credit may well lead to more demands by firms and other organized groups, and threaten the other achievements of reform so far. It is only one step from the use of credit to keep state firms alive to the reestablishment of price restrictions and controls to protect specific firms and groups in the population, a step that would eliminate much of the progress on price liberalization accomplished in 1992. If privatization means less de facto access to credit and subsidies, state firms may be reluctant to go private and privatization may slow down. The price signals under which privatization is taking place are fuzzy at best; the efficiency and wealth distribution implications may soon prove costly. These are the issues to watch for in the near future.

Privatization

Faced with the task of privatizing state firms, the first approach of Eastern European reform governments was to look at the methods that had been used in the West. It became quickly clear that this was not the right way: the task was too large, the information and bureaucratic requirements too burdensome. The second approach consisted of a set of plans aimed at finding the right tradeoff among speed, efficiency, and equity. There were many such, often ingenious plans; *Reform in Eastern Europe* sketched our own, based on reliance on the creation of transitional holding companies.

Two years later, reality has set in. Ambitious and clever plans have been disfigured by political compromises, bogged down in political fights, tied down by bureaucratic bottlenecks and foot dragging, sabotaged by those who would lose most from their implementation. The overall pace of privatization has been very slow. The basic lesson is clear: privatization is not about the distribution of assets belonging to "the state," which can dispose of them as it wishes, but about the distribution of assets with many de facto claimants: workers, managers, local authorities, central ministries, and so on. Unless these claimants are appeased, bribed, or disenfranchised, privatization cannot proceed. The main challenge of privatization is thus how to deal with and reconcile those claims. This is the issue we explore in chapter 3.

Nowhere are these conflicting claims more evident than in Russia. And the Russian privatization program starts squarely from the recognition of those claims, and of the relative power of the claimants. Who are these claimants? Pre-reform, they were ministries and managers. Ministries could affect delivery of scarce inputs, but only managers had the know-how required to make firms function. The collapse of central planning and the advent of reform have drastically changed the distribution of claims. Workers now have influence over employment, wages, and sometimes the choice of managers. They strongly feel that they have a large claim, sometimes even an exclusive claim to their firms. Managers on the other hand have remained very powerful, as their knowledge of the networks of suppliers and buyers is essential to running the firms. Both de jure and de facto, local governments have become more powerful and, with the strong support of their constituency, have also claimed a stake in firms under their jurisdiction. The major losers have been ministries, which are far from the firms and have lost their grip on the control of supplies.

Absent a privatization program, this new distribution of overlapping and conflicting claims is likely to lead to a continuation of the status quo. And because many of the stakeholders have enough effective control to veto any change, no restructuring can take place. This shows why privatization is essential. But it also shows why a program that establishes claims, and thus probably reduces some of them so that the sum of claims does not exceed one, may still be acceptable to all initial stakeholders: it is better to hold a smaller claim on a going concern than a larger claim on a paralyzed firm.

Based on this assessment, the Russian privatization program has been organized along the following lines. Workers and managers will get a lot. They have the choice at this point between three plans; in all three, they will receive at least a third of the shares, either free or at knock-down prices. Local authorities will get their share, but should get it mostly in the form of privatization proceeds, rather than control. That half of the labor force that works outside the enterprises to be privatized, and currently holds no claim, will also get something. This is being done through vouchers. Some 80–90 percent of the shares (other than those provided on preferential terms to workers and managers) will be auctioned for vouchers, the rest auctioned for cash. The distribution of vouchers was largely completed by the end of 1992; this precommits the government to find enterprises to sell. The ministries, which would very much want to form holding companies and to create a system of cross holdings, are, for the moment, getting little.

Privatization is proceeding along these lines. Many firms have been bought by insiders, at very low prices. These privatized firms are creating a strong constituency for reform. Many local auctions have been highly successful, yielding high prices and a strong temptation for local authorities to sell more firms, trading control for cash. Many things can obviously go wrong. Resources allocated to the privatization process are much too small. Those firms that are doing poorly but have access to credit do not want to be privatized. Ministries are not happy with current developments. But, at this point, privatization is proceeding quickly.

Trade and Payments Arrangements

1991 saw the collapse of trade among CMEA countries, 1992 the collapse of trade among the republics of the ex–Soviet Union. Central planning had led to an extraordinary degree of specialization of the republics. The most extreme example was perhaps Belarus, where trade with other republics was equal to more than 70 percent of the republic's net material product (NMP). This specialization makes the collapse of trade all the more worrisome.

Why has trade collapsed? Partly because of the reluctance of Russia and Russian firms to sell underpriced goods, such as oil, to other republics. Mostly because of the reluctance of the republics to accept rubles in exchange for goods. This has led firms to ask for payment in hard currency. But hard currency is in limited supply in most republics. And it has led to barter trade. But barter is an extraordinarily primitive way of conducting trade. For all these reasons, trade has declined, leading in turn to a decrease in output and further declines in trade.

The economists' answer to the problem is convertibility. Let all the republics have their own currency, and make their currency convertible, either at a fixed or, more likely, because of the lack of reserves, at a flexible rate. Movements in the exchange rate will solve the hard currency shortage, will solve any bilateral imbalance problem, and trade will increase. But many republics are not willing to consider full convertibility just yet. They are reluctant to accept the likely real depreciation that would come with convertibility, and they want to retain more control of foreign transactions than they would under convertibility. It is with that political constraint in mind that we explore, in chapter 4, the advantages of a payment mechanism.

Here is one very useful historical precedent, from Western Europe after World War II. Western Europe had emerged from the war with massive trade restrictions, and bilateral trade was the rule. A payments system was put in place, the European Payments Union, and was run by the Bank for International Settlements. It had two major functions.

The first was multilateral clearing of claims, with, each month, a statement of net credit or net debit for each country. This allowed countries with overall balanced trade to carry out transactions without the need to hold hard currency, and thus less of a need to generate hard currency earnings through transactions with the rest of the world.

The second was to relax the constraint that trade within the EPU be balanced each month. Each country was allocated a quota on its cumulative imbalances. When the country went beyond its quota, it had to settle an increasing portion in gold or dollars. Creditors in turn had to accept a portion of their net cumulative balance in credit, and the rest in gold or hard currency.

The system was supported politically by the US, which helped to capitalize it. It worked from 1950 to 1958, by which time most members had moved to full current account convertibility. The system was a success. We argue that a similar system could be set up at this point among the republics. It would not solve all problems. Exchange rates would still have to be set at levels consistent with balanced trade. And countries that ran large imbalances would still have to take the measures needed to prevent further imbalances. But it would eliminate the need for barter trade, save on the need for hard currency holdings, and allow interrepublic trade to recover. Central European countries, even those that have already established convertibility, would also gain from participating, as this would allow for trade between them and the republics without need for hard currency. And, like the US after the war, the West could both help set up and fund the system, giving it some leverage later in ensuring proper behavior of the participating republics.

Restructuring

Reform in Poland is now three years old. Stabilization has been achieved, at least for the time being. The central issues are now those of restructuring, of how to close those state firms that need to be closed, of how to successfully transform those that should survive, and of how to foster and protect the growth of the new private sector. These are the issues we deal with in chapter 5.

Three preconditions are essential to the success of restructuring.

The first is price liberalization, so that prices provide the right incentives to firms and to consumers. This was largely achieved early on in the reform process.

The second is the hardening of the "soft budget constraint," so that market signals are not offset by subsidies or confiscatory taxation. In sharp contrast to Russia, credibility on this front was also achieved early on. This credibility has been tested a few times, especially in the first half of 1992, when it appeared that the newly formed government might be more sympathetic to the plight of struggling state firms. But it has survived, and firms are now accepting the realities of hard budget constraints.

The third is privatization, so that firms have the right incentives to respond to market signals. There, as we discussed earlier, progress has been very slow. The reasons are many. Initial plans, and even those that followed, were too complex. Many of the power plays now taking place in Russia were carried out either within the Polish government or in Parliament, leading to long debates and longer delays. The bureaucracies in charge have had strong incentives to err on the side of prudence, thus of inaction. As a result, the large majority of state firms is still in ownership limbo. If everything goes right, the most ambitious plan to date, "mass privatization," will clear Parliament during the first quarter of 1993.

In the absence of privatization, the magnitude of the restructuring task, together with uncertainty about their stake in the restructured firm, have led managers and workers in state firms to act with short horizons. Without changes in incentives, most state firms are now behaving passively unless threatened with extinction, acting to avoid immediate closure but rarely willing or able to take the measures needed to survive and grow.

Private sector growth, on the other hand, has been impressive. Including agriculture, private sector employment now accounts for about half of total employment. Growth has been highest in those sectors that had traditionally been repressed, trade and services. That the Polish economy needed more of those is not at issue. But, given how little restructuring has happened in state firms in manufacturing, the question arises of whether and to what extent growth of the private sector can substitute for the restructuring of state firms. The answer is that private firms clearly cannot be expected, any time soon, to substitute for the transformation of existing state firms. Modern manufacturing is too large and too sophisticated to be developed quickly from scratch, especially with limited foreign participation.

The process of restructuring is proceeding. Employment in state firms has stabilized, and the worst appears over. But partial paralysis of the state sector and uneven development of the private sector imply that the process can easily derail. The contraction and the disappearance of profits in state firms have led to a chronic fiscal crisis. Deficits have been kept under control, but the danger is always there. With prospects of many state firms becoming increasingly somber, political pressure for subsidies will also grow. Again, this pressure has been resisted until now; but it will not go away. The two most urgent items on the agenda are faster privatization, to change the dynamics of behavior in the state sector, and the reform of the banking system, to allow saving to go where it is most needed.

2   Stabilization versus Reform? Russia's First Year

In 1992 Russia rediscovered capitalism—one of the main events of the century. Yet many people say the reforms have failed, since inflation is still rampant.

This line of thought is flawed. For the aim of the Russian reform is to change from communism to capitalism. Price stability is something else—one of the aims of any government, communist or capitalist.

Price stability is more difficult to achieve in a free society than in a command economy. Under communism, so long as state power is intact, wages can be regulated and strikes forbidden. This makes it possible to contain inflation even when everyone is guaranteed a job. But in free societies inflation can only be controlled with a certain amount of unemployment.

Thus, during the economic transition, inflation inevitably increases unless unemployment is allowed to rise. In most

---

Written by Richard Layard.

countries of Eastern Europe inflation was contained because unemployment was allowed to rise from the very beginning of the reform. So far this has not happened in Russia. One year after the reform began unemployment was only 1.3 percent, and inflation was 25 percent per month.

Was this an error of judgment on the part of the reformers? Almost certainly not. Of course the Gaidar team would have preferred a tighter credit policy and less inflation. But this would have meant more unemployment, and the aversion to unemployment in Russia is far deeper than in Eastern Europe, due to 70 years of totally secure employment. And the military-industrial complex, where unemployment would strike heavily, is strong and menacing.

The Gaidar team's main aim was to privatize the economy. If they had also attempted an early stabilization, they would have been thrown from office within months. They compromised, because of the tradeoffs they faced.

First, there is the economic tradeoff between unemployment and inflation: the control of inflation would have come at the cost of unemployment (figure 2.1a).[1] In the East, where unemployment starts from zero, major falls in output are an inevitable consequence of stabilization, and the need to restructure adds further to the problem. The word recession is inappropriate. It is also quite absurd to call these falls in output a failure of the supply response. They are an inevitable first step in adjusting to a market economy.

(a) Unemployment and extra inflation (economic tradeoff)

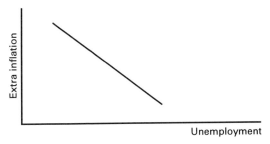

(b) Privatization and extra inflation (political tradeoff)

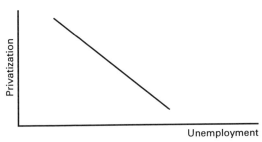

Hence, (c) Privatization and extra inflation

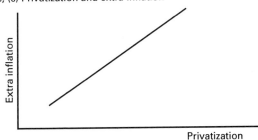

Figure 2.1
Tradeoffs facing the Gaidar government.

But then there is the political tradeoff: extra unemployment will undermine the government and thus reduce the chances of privatization (figure 2.1b). Hence in order to privatize, the government will have to accept some inflation (figure 2.1c). Whereas in the West governments can focus on the choice between inflation and unemployment, in Russia any reforming government must also allow for the politics of privatization. In their first year the Gaidar government chose to remain in power in order to build a private enterprise economy, even though this meant high inflation.

No attempt was made to stabilize the price level. Since this part of the full reform package has not yet been tried, it cannot be said to have failed. By contrast, the reforms that have been attempted have gone well. Price liberalization has been remarkably successful, and commercialization and privatization have proceeded at good speed.

For the West the key issue is whether Russia can successfully make the complete transition. We therefore begin this chapter by appraising the record to date. After a brief historical review, we address directly the major criticisms that have been made: that the liberalization was too quick and the output fall excessive. Finally we examine the special features of Russia in world society and ask what the West can do.

We do not offer a full description of what has happened, which can be found in the government's quarterly report, *Russian Economic Trends*, and in analyses by the World Bank

(1992) and by Lipton and Sachs (1992).[2] But we do include a statistical appendix at the end of this volume, with graphs that tell the tale.

Brief Chronicle

The reform government was formed in November 1991. On 2 January most prices were freed from central government control, except for prices for energy and transport. Due to the huge monetary overhang, prices rose by 250 percent within a few days, increasing the velocity of circulation of M2 from 0.15 times per month to 0.44 (a fairly typical Western value). Wages rose very much less, so that real wages fell to about $\frac{2}{3}$ of their 1985 level. This led to a drastic fall in consumption.

At the same time there was a major pruning of the budget. Subsidies were slashed and military procurement was cut to $\frac{1}{8}$ of its former level. The budget deficit fell from some 20 percent of GDP in 1991 to around 5 percent in the first half of 1992. This sequence in turn affected investment purchases, which fell by a half.

At first output did not respond to the fall in demand, and enterprises continued to produce at the old rate, accumulating massive stocks. In many cases this stock building was deliberate: given negative real interest rates, it made sense to charge high prices and accumulate goods rather than rubles. But, given a degree of credit rationing, enterprises found it difficult to finance their stocks and stopped paying their bills. Interenterprise debt rose to around $2\frac{1}{2}$ months' GNP.

By April enterprises started cutting production and by the summer industrial production was down a quarter on a year earlier. By this stage the clamor for easy credit became deafening: credit to pay off the arrears, to "index working capital," and above all to "stabilize production."

Following on the April meeting of the Congress of People's Deputies, the reform government had been diluted by the addition of four deputy prime ministers with industrial background, and an old-guard governor had been appointed to the Central Bank. The Bank and the government made big concessions to the clamor for credit.

This was a major reversal of policy. Up to May monetary growth had been fairly steady at under 15 percent per month. Since velocity fell slightly, the result was a steady price inflation of around 10 percent per month from May to September. But from June to August there was a large emission of credit, with credits from the Central Bank growing at over 40 percent per month. This led to a temporary halt to the fall in production from August to the end of the year. This process in turn intensified inflationary pressure, and inflation rose to 25 percent per month from October onward and into the new year.

In December, Yegor Gaidar was succeeded by a more conservative prime minister, Viktor Chernomyrdin, but the direction of economic policy was left under a reformer. At the time of writing the new government was deciding its strategy.

Thus in 1992 macroeconomic control over inflation was not established. But, beneath the high inflation, microeconomic change proceeded apace. The privatization program was agreed by Parliament in June and is discussed in chapter 3. Even before privatization, the budget squeeze had a major effect in making enterprises take responsibility for their own destinies. But the greatest source of change in the first year was the program of liberalization.

Was Liberalization Too Quick?

Critics inside and outside Russia have argued that the liberalization was too quick. Let us begin with the price liberalization.

Prices

The aim in freeing prices is to eliminate excess demand. Excess demand wastes millions of hours in queuing and searching. It leads sellers to disregard the interests of customers. And it leads to an inappropriate pattern of supply.

Russia's price liberalization has hugely reduced the queues. And it has led to perceptible improvements in the quality of service and the physical appearance of the shops. But one should not exaggerate the changes, which have if anything been too little.

Liberalization has not eliminated the mafia, but neither did it create it. The mafia flourishes in a two-price system where privileged people buy at low prices and sell illegally at high ones. These opportunities have been significantly reduced. But anybody with the power to prevent the movement of goods can always extract a rent. This power will unfortunately continue in Russia for some time until legitimate forms of state power are reestablished.

One should not exaggerate the degree of deregulation that has happened in Russia. Local authorities can still regulate prices, provided they pay the necessary subsidies out of their local budgets. Thus shortages of some goods still persist in some areas. More serious, much trade is still directed by state orders. In mid-1992 some 40 percent of interenterprise trade was still directed rather than market-based, and some 40 percent of agricultural output was subject to compulsory procurement (Aslund 1992). Shops are limited to 25 percent markups, which still leads to enormously inefficient petty trading on the streets. Thus, if anything, the liberalization has been too little rather than too much. The much criticized "speculators" on the streets are still exploiting the two-price system, which would disappear under complete liberalization.

But wasn't price liberalization meant to generate a supply response? In one sense yes, but in another sense no. The first aim of the liberalization was to eliminate excess demand. This inevitably required an initial fall in economic activity, not an increase. But in due course there must, of course, be higher productivity, and thus a better level and structure of output. Free prices are meant to guide the economy to the new structure.

Foreign trade

This means taking proper advantage of the opportunities for international trade, which means liberalizing it. People often ask why convertibility is so important for Russia when Europe did all right without it for so long after 1945. The answer is that, if you have been cut off for so long, it is much more important to be in touch with other peoples' know-how than when the isolation has been brief, as during a war.

Foreign trade is also the best antidote to monopoly power. Some critics argued that Russia should not have liberalized its prices until it had demonopolized.[3] But this would have meant an intolerable delay. Far better to free domestic prices *and* to free foreign trade.

This Russia has been doing steadily but surely. Even in 1991 importers could buy foreign exchange freely in a weekly auction. But the market was very thin. The key practical issue regarding convertibility is a quantitative one: how much of the nation's foreign exchange earnings are being sold to importers at the market rate and how much allocated at below the market rate. By early autumn about half of foreign exchange was allocated at the market rate to enterprises producing certificates of import, while the rest went for centralized imports at way below market rates. In these cases the government bought the foreign exchange at the market price and subsidized the price difference.[4]

There is thus a high degree of current account convertibility. Even though enterprises cannot buy dollars except for purposes of importing, there is also a considerable de facto capital account convertibility. This is because exporters are allowed to sell anything between 50 and 100 percent of their foreign exchange earnings, giving them considerable latitude in their portfolio choice.

Many Russians (Petrakov et al. 1992) have blamed convertibility for the inflation. The argument is that a floating exchange rate (with limited sales of foreign exchange) brought down the value of the ruble, and Russian prices then moved upward in response to the rise in import prices. In fact however the ruble was very stable in the first half of the year and the subsequent fall was caused by monetary policy (rather than monetary policy accommodating some speculative fall in the ruble).

Even so, government thinking has been unduly influenced by the fear that world influences would have an inflationary impact on Russia. Thus de facto price control has been in force for all raw materials (including grain). The method is the export quota. Since May the price of oil and all other raw materials has been essentially determined by the demand price for the supplies available on the Russian market. The export quotas have held down the relative price of raw materials in Russia. But they have probably had little effect on the average domestic price level, which has been determined by monetary forces.

Higher energy prices would make possible an energy tax, with excellent effects on the budget and thus on money, as well as higher investment in energy production. And larger energy exports would increase the flow of foreign exchange, improving the value of the ruble. Thus in trade liberalization, as in price liberalization, there has been if anything too little liberalization, rather than too much.

Did Output Fall Too Much?

Even so, output has fallen considerably. During 1991, before the reform, industrial production fell by 15 percent. During 1992 it fell by 23 percent—some indication of the impact of the reform. Why did production fall so much, and was the fall too great, as Petrakov (1992), Yavlinsky (1992), and others have argued?

Causes

As Table 2.1 shows, GDP fell by a fifth or more in almost every Eastern European country in the three years after

Table 2.1
Changes in GDP (%)

	1990	1991	1992	Cumulative
Poland	−12	−9	−2	−22
Hungary	−3	−10	−4	−16
Czechoslovakia	—	−16	−7	−22
Bulgaria	−9	−17	−10	−32
Romania	−7	−14	−13	−30
Former USSR	−4	−17	−18	−35

Source: OECD, *Economic Outlook*, December 1992, p. 126. 1992 data estimated.

democracy dawned. And in most countries almost all manufacturing industries declined.

The fact is striking because the circumstances of the countries were very varied. Some of the largest falls occurred in 1990 before the breakup of the CMEA. There must therefore be a central common cause: freedom itself. When workers can strike and producers can fix their own prices, everything changes. Inflationary forces are unleashed that, if they meet with any degree of fiscal and monetary restraint, cause falls in real demand and then falls in output.

This is why the so-called Chinese option is not available. In China strikes are still illegal and substantial price controls can be enforced because state power is still upheld through the mechanism of the Communist Party. In these circumstances a degree of reform can be achieved without a fall in output (Hussain and Stern 1991). This alternative is no longer available in Eastern Europe nor in Russia, where the collapse of central control has been a key feature of the last two years.

Thus in Russia output fell through the interaction between inflationary pressures (generated by the Phillips curve) and financial policies that were only partly accommodating. One particular manifestation of restraint was of course the cutback in military procurement, which had strong flow-back effects on the rest of the economy. But the single largest fall in demand and output was for consumer goods, stemming from price liberalization and the ending of most food subsidies.

The collapse of the CMEA at the end of 1990 and of the Soviet Union at the end of 1991 have been further contributory causes. Russia's exports (outside the former Soviet Union) fell from $81 billion in 1990 to $52 billion and around $34 billion in the following two years, the biggest fall being in exports to CMEA countries. Imports fell roughly in line with this. Foreign trade decline caused output to fall not mainly because exports fell but because (with trade balanced) there was a consequent cutback in complementary imports. As regards interrepublic trade, there is very little data, but trade may well have been halved.

It is very important to devise arrangements to restore trade, since many (but not all) of the trade linkages that have been disrupted were natural and healthy. In chapter 4 we put forward some suggestions.

But what else, if anything, should be done to restore production? There are a number of key points. First, the best

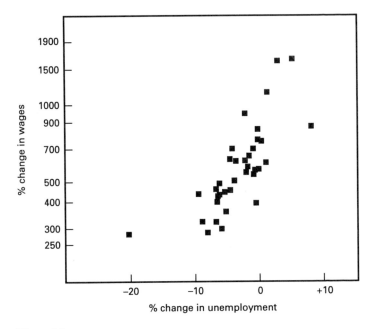

Figure 2.2
Wage and employment changes across industrial sectors: changes in 38
industries from January–February 1991 to January–February 1992. Source:
Ellam and Layard (1993).

way to promote production is to promote productivity. In
the West it is the level of employment that determines the
degree of inflationary pressure, and the same appears to be
true in Russia (see figure 2.2). Thus there has to be enough
unemployment to control inflation. But we want the output
per person employed to be as high as possible.

This is where performance in Eastern Europe has been so
disappointing. As unemployment has risen, the productivity of those employed has fallen sharply. When enterprises

have seen their output fall by x percent, they have typically reduced employment by almost one-fifth of x percent.[5] Thus unemployment has risen much less than output has fallen (see table 2.2).

This contrasts strongly with the behavior of enterprises in Spain and Germany during their periods of liberalization (around 1978 and 1948 respectively). In both countries unemployment rose quite sharply (see table 2.3). But there was no hoarding of unproductive labor. The hoarding seen in Eastern Europe and Russia simply reflects the absence of profit-oriented owners of the enterprise. This is one reason why Russian privatization is so urgent. If living standards are not to be reduced a lot further, it is vital that those workers who are employed be producing things, and producing things that people want.

This means that, when the old industries decline, new activities must develop. There is ample opportunity for extra

Table 2.2
Unemployment (%, end of year)

	1990	1991	1992
Poland	6	12	15
Hungary	2	8	13
Czechoslovakia	1	7	8
Bulgaria	2	12	15
Romania	—	3	6
Former USSR	0	1	2

Source: OECD, *Economic Outlook*, December 1992, p. 126. 1992 data estimated.

Table 2.3
Productivity Change after Stabilization

Years after stabili- zation	Poland (year 0 = 1990)		Spain (year 0 = 1978)		Germany (year 0 = 1948)	
	Unemploy- ment	Industrial produc- tivity	Unemploy- ment	Industrial produc- tivity	Unemploy- ment	Industrial produc- tivity
0	0	100	7	100	4	100
1	3	84	8	102	8	120
2	8	73	11	106	10	140

Source: OECD.

jobs in retailing, where Russia employs less than half the normal Western numbers (Lipton and Sachs, table 3). Business services too will grow, though one hopes at the expense of other branches of administration.

It is, however, easy to exaggerate the size of Russian manufacturing. Only 30 percent of Russian workers are in manufacturing—fairly similar to the situation in Western Europe. Military production appears to have employed only some 5 percent of the workforce. Russia is of course a major raw material producer and can therefore run a trade deficit in manufactures. But, as in the British case, this argument can be overdone. It is also difficult to transfer workers from manufacturing to other sectors, especially when they live in towns or cities dominated by a single manufacturing enterprise.

Unemployment beyond say 15 percent has little further influence in controlling inflation. So it makes no sense to let unemployment in any city rise above the level. Moreover the political consequences of mass unemployment could be very serious.

The continuation of the reform thus has two key ingredients: a sufficient rise in unemployment to control inflation, plus enough positive developments to maintain support for a reform government. It is difficult to see how the second element can possibly be achieved without Western support.

Russia and the West

If the West is to play a major role, this will have to start from the premise that Russia is different, so that an explicitly political approach is needed.

Western Self-Interest

Western self-interest is much more heavily involved than in the case of any other aid recipient. Russia is a heavily armed superpower. Under President Yeltsin it has had an exceptionally peace-loving government, which has abandoned an empire with even more grace than the British. This process cannot be just assumed to continue.

Russia is also a major arms producer that, if the country becomes disordered or economically desperate, could destabilize almost any part of the world by organized or unsupervised arms sales, including sales of nuclear weapons.

Russia is also a potentially rich country, rich in mineral deposits and in human capital. We know it could prosper within the foreseeable future well enough to service existing and future debts. Such a country should be allowed to borrow.

But there is a far wider externality problem. Future prosperity requires the policies to work out all right, which in turn requires sufficient initial success. If Russia receives little help, even that help may be wasted.

Russia's Political Difficulties

Unfortunately in 1991 and 1992 the West adopted a wait-and-see attitude to Russia. The International Monetary Fund was charged by the group of seven major industrial countries (G7) to act as their adviser, and the IMF felt obliged in the interest of consistency to apply to Russia the same criteria that it would apply to any potential creditor. The IMF gave no weight (at least initially) to Russia's superpower role nor to the finely balanced political situation in Russia—with a unique opportunity provided by the new reform government.[6] The attitude was that Russia should receive money when it had shown that it had the ability to stabilize its inflation.

However, in practice Russia never had the ability to stabilize without massive foreign assistance. There was thus a chicken-and-egg problem. If Russia received billions, this would lead to a real appreciation that would improve the Phillips curve tradeoff between unemployment and extra inflation. This in turn might make possible a stabilization.

But in all honesty one cannot be sure that even with a better Phillips curve Russia could have stabilized, so great were the pressures to sustain output to the limits where hyperinflation threatens.

This was because of the dreadful constitutional tangle in Russia. The Congress was elected in March 1990 while the Communist Party still ruled, and, though other candidates were allowed, 87 percent of those elected were CP members. The Congress did not reflect the current opinions of the people. For example, by January 1992 three-quarters of the population favored individual ownership of land, which was strenuously opposed by the Congress (Lipton and Sachs 1992). And even in September 1992, 49 percent of the population thought the pace of reforms should be speeded up—reforms the Congress was busy slowing down (Aslund 1992).

So what should the West have concluded? It could not affect the constitutional tangle but it should have acted strongly to enable Yeltsin to show some positive results from reform. The most important result to achieve was not macroeconomic stability (low inflation) but microeconomic progress. To push forward the restructuring (and to silence his industrial critics), Yeltsin desperately needed funds with which to help Russian industries modify their production in order to capture new markets. This meant critical imports of machinery and imputs. It was a situation very similar to that in post–World War II Europe. Postwar Europe was also politically unstable. The Marshall Plan provided a limited amount of foreign aid, which helped to promote new growth. It surely made a difference (DeLong and Eichengreen 1993). Though its relevance cannot be proved, the contrast between Germany after World War II and Germany after World War I is striking and ominous.

Russia needed and still needs something like a Marshall Plan organized through an office with strong microeconomic orientations based in Moscow. The money would be lent to the Russian government and lent on by them to enterprises, in most cases at realistic rates.[7] Criteria for resource allocation should be economic, which would include some allowance for shadow wage costs (below market levels) in high unemployment areas.

Some of the funds need of course to be used for infrastructure projects and the promotion of public goods such as information. For example there needs to be a major drive for promoting exports of Russian manufacturers, if a tragedy is to be avoided in many industrial centers. The Russian domestic market will be subdued, but many Russian goods are potentially supercompetitive in world markets. In Russia skilled labor is among the cheapest in the world, with graduate engineers paid under $10 a month. This general pattern will prevail for some years. Russia has already many excellent products. Even if the final product is military, or a civilian product not satisfying Western standards or tastes, the components may be excellent and available at bargain prices. Many of these goods are not being exported. No one buys them because no one knows they are there; there is here an information failure that requires a direct frontal assault. Aid money used to promote Russian exports has great leverage and provides real hope that the human casualties of stabilization will work again.

Similar arguments apply to infrastructure investment in privatization and commercial training.[8] But the bulk of the money should go directly to enterprises on commercial terms.

So what of stabilization? At some point the Russian public will become more averse to inflation than to unemployment. In readiness the West has to stand by with a stabilization fund and some general balance of payments support (dollars for sale in the market). In the meantime it is nonsense to suppose that Russia cannot use targeted aid to good effect, even if inflation remains high.

Conclusion

After 70 years of communism and one year only of democratic rule, it is inevitable that the reform process in Russia is difficult. Compromises have to be made to keep the reform moving.

Democracy rules out the Chinese solution. Once workers can go on strike, the inflationary pressure associated with full employment is uncontrollable except by a process of rising unemployment. Thus President Yeltsin is treading a narrow path between hyperinflation and politically unacceptable layoffs. With more positive help from the West, this path could be widened and the prospects for freedom and peace improved.

3   The Politics of Russian Privatization

On July 3, 1991, the Russian legislature passed a law that mandated privatizing most state firms and prescribed methods for doing so. The work on implementation of this law was slow at first, and was interrupted by momentous changes in the government in August. Starting from mid-November of 1991, the new government resumed the work on privatization guidelines. On December 27, 1991, the Supreme Soviet passed an elaboration of the July 3 law, called the "Fundamental Positions of the Privatization Program." In January 1992, this document was supplemented by several decrees signed by Boris Yeltsin that explained the various steps of the process. Finally, in late March 1992, the government produced the actual privatization program that it offered to the Russian Parliament for approval. After much controversy and negotiation, the Parliament accepted the program on June 11, 1992. This chapter describes the privatization program and the political influences that shaped it. In particular, we focus on one key issue that the privatization program confronted: how to reconcile the

Written by Andrei Shleifer and Maxim Boycko.

conflicting claims of the de facto "owners" of assets that must be privatized?

The issue of the initial allocation of property rights in state firms, before they are privatized, rarely receives attention. In many cases, it simply does not arise. For example, in the UK privatization, the government clearly owned the shares it sold, and so there was no question of who was selling the shares, only how and to whom. Even in the context of Eastern Europe, it is often simply assumed that the government owns the shares and then has to sell or distribute them to the population. The questions that generate intellectual and practical excitement are, first, who should be the eventual owners of the shares, and, second, how to sell or allocate the shares from the government to these eventual owners to maximize efficiency? Both of these questions presume that the seller of shares is clear, namely the government.

Yet as the experience of Poland illustrates, the workers of the companies do not agree that the shares are the government's to distribute as it wishes. Failure to appreciate this point is undoubtedly an important cause of the delay of privatization in Poland. Companies in Eastern Europe in general, and Russia in particular, do not have an unambiguous de facto ownership structure, in which the government owns the shares. On the contrary, many "stakeholders" have existing ownership rights, *in the sense of being able to effectively exercise control rights over assets.*

Moreover, these stakeholders take both economic and political action to defend their rights. Unless these stakeholders are appeased, bribed, or disenfranchised, privatization cannot proceed.

In Poland and Hungary, the important stakeholders are the workers and the managers. In Russia the workers and particularly the managers are also extremely influential, but the local governments and the branch ministries also play a role. These stakeholders correctly see privatization as a redistribution of property rights rather than as a gift from the government. The question that the privatization program has to address are how the center can reconcile the control claims of these multiple de facto owners, and how it can reduce the damage they do while competing for the pie. The program reflects these efforts to reconcile the stakeholders.

This chapter first surveys the distribution of property rights in enterprises under socialism, and shows how the relatively clear distribution of these rights collapses when socialism does. The decline of the power of the state and the ministries has created an ownership vacuum in Russia that has been filled by new effective owners: the workers, the managers, and the local governments, whose control rights are often in conflict. We then discuss the privatization program as an effort to reconcile the conflicting claims on the assets, and examine the likely future of the Russian privatization, focusing on the possible areas of success and failure.

Ownership during Socialism and after Its Collapse

Ownership under Socialism

Under socialism, the state supposedly owns all the means
of production, including the firms. This notion of ownership, however, is not particularly revealing. Ownership con-
sists of a claim to residual profits as well as to residual
control rights (Grossman and Hart 1986). The treasury has
some claim on profits or losses of state firms. But there is
no "state" that has control rights. These rights instead are
shared by the managers of the firm and the bureaucrats in
the ministry that oversees the firm. The ministry bureaucrats are probably the more important owners, in the sense
of having most of the power to dictate the decisions of the
firms. Legally, the ministry bureaucrats have the right to
choose the top managers, to determine the production and
investment, to set prices, to allocate inputs and buy outputs,
to determine the general growth rate of wages, and so on.
They do not make micro production decisions, but they
control most of the other ones. Most rights of the ministry
bureaucrats are enforced through central control, but they
also maintain these rights through complete control over
the delivery of scarce inputs.

How do the ministry bureaucrats translate these control rights into cash flows for themselves? The ministry
bureaucrats use their rights to extract surplus from the
firm, subject to attaining some minimal level of profits
(or maximal level of losses) for the treasury. One way

to do it is to extract presents and services from the firm. Another way to extract surplus is to underprice the supplier's and the firm's output. By intentionally making the inputs scarce, the bureaucrats can extract bribes from the firm in exchange for deliveries; by making outputs scarce, they can do the same with the firm's customers. Pervasive shortages under socialism result from this profit-maximizing exercise by the bureaucrats of their effective ownership rights.

Under socialism, managers of the firm also have some control rights. They have the know-how and the connections to solve the problems of pervasive shortages and breakdowns. This gives them some control over production, investment, and employment decisions, as well as over most micro decisions of firms. Their knowledge also makes them valuable to the bureaucrats, and hence enables them to collect some of the rents from the firm.

In contrast, workers own nothing under socialism—Marx and Lenin notwithstanding. Workers own the firm only to the extent that they have an influence over its policies or a claim on its cash flows. In communist Russia, workers' ability to strike and otherwise exercise control rights was severely limited by the central government. They certainly had no control over wages or employment. Also relatively unimportant were the local governments: any attempt by them to exercise control over the firm was certain to invite retribution from the center. With full control over local budgets, the center had local governments under its thumb. The relevant owners, then, were first the ministry bureaucrats and second the managers.

Ownership during the Transition

The control rights over the decisions of firms have changed radically in Russia since 1988, as socialism and central control have collapsed. Starting in 1988, the government implemented a range of reforms that transferred many of the decisions over output mix, output level, customer choice, and wages to enterprise managers. The ministries also lost their right to appoint managers, although it is not clear who gained it (the workers began to have some input). The 1988 reforms kept the prices fixed, but at the same time allowed firms to sell a small portion of their output at free prices. The reforms also kept most of the input allocation centralized, thereby letting the ministries keep most of their effective control rights.

Over the subsequent three years, the ability of the center to enforce the planned allocation has collapsed. The Communist Party had enforced deliveries to the state, and that mechanism simply failed. As a result, enterprises refused to deliver their products to the state at low prices, and instead began selling them at market prices to whomever they pleased. What began as a Chinese-style experiment with capitalism on the margin transformed itself into a collapse of the central allocation mechanisms. This collapse of socialist coordination greatly damaged state enterprises and may have led to aggregate output declines in 1990 and 1991.

These changes deprived the ministries of most of their control rights. First, they could no longer dictate to firms what to do, and even if they tried they had no law or force to support their orders. More importantly, when the ministries lost control over the outputs of some enterprises, they also lost control over firms for which these outputs were inputs. When the ministries could no longer assure supply deliveries, managers had to find inputs, which often meant barter and other market transactions. To the extent that the control rights of the ministries depended on supply assurance, these control rights have diminished a great deal.

The control rights of the ministries have not disappeared completely. Because ministries still have control over some industry assets, such as research institutes, information networks, and export licenses, they continue to exercise control over firms. Perhaps more importantly, branch ministers from the old regime continue to sit on the council of ministers, and in fact have more votes in the aggregate than do the members of the reform team. They use this power to influence the course of privatization in two main directions. First, they argue that many state firms are too vital to be privatized or even to be transferred to the jurisdiction of the local governments. The ministries want to keep government control over assets because control brings the ability to extract cash flow and services from these firms in the future, as well as continuation of ministerial jobs.

Second, if privatization is to take place, the ministers want it to take the form of free distribution of shares among firms in the same industry, their suppliers, and customers. Moreover, the ministries insist that they actually supervise this allocation of shares and hold some of the shares. They would like to form holding companies that are organized by the ministries and often hold controlling blocks of shares in the enterprises, while enterprises themselves hold shares in the holding company. Thus, according to some plans, the managers and workers of each enterprise would get 30 percent of the shares, and the remainder would be held by suppliers, customers, and the ministerial holding company. Many important ministers, including Vladimir Shumeiko, the first deputy prime minister, support privatization plans along these lines. The ostensible reason for such privatization is to preserve supply links and to avert the further collapse of the economy. It is obvious, however, that preserving the existing supply relationships through cross holdings and holding companies is largely a way to preserve existing industrial structures and ministerial oversight and not to allow any outsiders to exercise any control rights. The ministers thus accept privatization only if it preserves their control over firms.

As the bureaucrats partly lost their control over enterprises, who gained it? In Russia, this control has reverted to stakeholders who previously had very little power. These stakeholders include the workers of the firm, the local governments, and most importantly the enterprise managers. To understand who de facto owns the firms before privatization begins, we must clarify the control rights of these stakeholders.

Consider first the workers. Today, the workers have influence over employment, wages, and sometimes the choice of managers. After liberalization, the workers got a right to negotiate collective bargaining agreements and to strike. This and the influence over the choice of managers give them control over employment and wages. Even where the workers do not select the managers, managers recognize that privatization will in many cases formally allocate voting rights to the workers tomorrow. This, of course, gives the workers many effective control rights today. Perhaps most importantly, the privatization program requires that privatization plans of all enterprises be approved by the workers' collectives. No matter how little power the workers will have after privatization, the managers must get them to go along with the privatization plan. This gives workers some power in the meantime.

In addition to these economic sources of worker power, workers represent a substantial number of voters, in the Russian as well as local elections. The democratic political process thus naturally favors the allocation of the control rights over the firms' assets to the workers. In the Parliament, the deputies who claim to represent workers' interest are numerous and powerful. It is not entirely clear whether these deputies actually represent the workers, or whether they simply reflect the interests of the managers and use the workers as an excuse (much as in the case of trade protection). After all, managers end up being substantial beneficiaries of most regulations that are alleged to benefit the workers. Whatever its true motivations, the workers' lobby is quite powerful in the Parliament, and the privatization program contains many benefits for the workers reflecting these pressures. Without doubt, compared to the regime prior to reforms, changes in Russia have led to a large increase in the control rights of workers—similar though not as dramatic as what has occurred in Poland.

Workers and their supporters have expressed very strong claims on the assets of the state firms. Worker groups have demanded 100 percent ownership of the assets of their firms. Larisa Pyasheva, the head of the Moscow privatization program, has formally endorsed this strategy of giving everything free to the workers as rapid and fair. The July 3 privatization law allows for a sale of some government shares to workers at a 30 percent discount, and the actual privatization program has actually gone much further, as we discuss below. But the initial demands of the advocates of worker ownership have been much more extreme. An interesting illustration along these lines is that of VAZ, the giant automobile manufacturer that has been negotiating a sale of 33 percent of its shares to Fiat for a price between $1 billion and $2.5 billion. The proceeds from the sale are to be invested in upgrading VAZ. In late November 1991, the workers of VAZ addressed an open letter to Yeltsin and the prime minister of Italy, demanding that they immediately get a 51 percent share in VAZ before any discussions of sale take place, and that some of the revenues from the sale be allocated to them as shareholders. They have also threatened industrial action should their demand be rejected. Since the Fiat investment is the best hope for these workers regardless of whether they own any shares, their demands are a clear illustration of the vastly increased control rights of the Russian workers. As of this writing, VAZ is apparently concentrating on a worker-management buyout (rather than a sale to foreigners) at a very low price, which would greatly enrich VAZ workers and make its managers dollar multimillionaires. The Russian government, of course, would get much less than it would from Fiat.

This brings us to the most important constituency whose control rights have increased tremendously since 1988, namely the managers. First, the existing law gives managers a lot of discretion over what to produce, what price to charge, and whom to sell the output to. The legal control rights over firms are therefore largely theirs. Second, even when the ministries have retained legal rights, they are no longer obeyed and hence the control rights by default revert to the managers. If anything, the ministries now depend for their survival on contributions from the state firms. Managers also have some control rights over employment and wages, which conflict with the control rights of the workers on these decisions. Finally, the managers have the network of contacts and the personal relationships that are essential for barter and for the procurement of inputs. They have thus inherited from the bureaucrats their most important control right.

Like the workers, managers have been trying to use their political influence, with the local governments, the Parliament, and now inside the Yeltsin cabinet, to translate the effective control into the ownership of cash flows as well. The usual strategy of the managers is to hide behind the workers, and to insist on greater benefits for the workers' collectives. Typically, this means worker-management buy-outs at a low (and sometimes zero) price, where managers often get large ownership stakes and complete control in exchange for promising high wages to the workers. Managers also prefer these buyouts to take a partnership rather than a corporate form, mostly to avoid possible control challenges in the future. In other cases, where the managers do not see an opportunity to profitably buy out the company—say in the military or some other clearly bankrupt industry—they join forces with branch ministries and advocate the formation of ministerial holding companies, with the resulting preservation of the managers' positions and of soft budget constraints. It is fair to say that most opposition to the government's privatization program has come from the managers' lobby, and has taken the form of either supporting the holdings or demanding greater benefits for the workers, i.e., the managers.

Last but not least, the local governments also gained many new control rights. After the demise of the Communist Party and of the central control over government more generally, the local governments have found tremendous room to govern their localities. Because the local governments are typically democratically elected, they have some legitimacy as representatives of the local population. In addition, they have received control over some key local assets, such as electricity, water, and other utilities, and can translate this control into influence over firms.

Not surprisingly, the local governments have demanded a share of the revenues of the enterprises in their areas, particularly in the areas rich in oil and other natural resources. They have also demanded and received a say over who the firms can enter joint ventures with, what they can produce, and what they can barter. Many localities have gone on to demand that large state enterprises be made responsible for the procurement of foodstuffs for all the residents in their areas. They have also tried to change firms' policies toward pollution and other public goods. Many of the control rights of the ministries have thus been transferred to the local governments.

In the privatization area, the local governments have demanded both the right to privatize and the revenues from privatization. Since December 1991, the Moscow city government and the Russian government have fought over the speed and the mechanism of privatization in Moscow. In demanding all these control rights, the local governments realize the inability of the center to enforce Russian laws. They also make effective threats: to turn off water and electricity at factories that do not cooperate. Even more effective are the threats from the republics on Russian territory inhabited by ethnic minorities to declare independence unless they receive control over firms on their territories. But the most serious problem is that the local governments often do not want to privatize at all. Instead, they want to use prospective privatization as a mechanism to transfer control over firms from the ministries to themselves, so that they can continue the upravleniye, or management, on their own. In many cases, the ability of the local governments to assure the supply of goods to their areas, as well as power and bribes for themselves, relies on retaining control over firms rather than privatizing them.

The remaining stakeholder in the Russian firms in the Russian "state," the nominal owner of these assets. Traditionally, the state exercised its control rights through the ministries and the Communist Party. In light of the decline of both, the state has no clear residual control rights at all, although it nominally has all the residual cash flow rights.

Formally, the state is represented in the privatization process by GKI, the State Committee on Property. This committee is supposed to oversee privatization and take care of the state property before it is privatized. While the committee is quite small, it is supposed to have regional representatives who do its job in various regions. In practice, the local governments have already demanded control over appointing the local representatives of GKI, even though GKI is an explicitly federal organization. The functioning of the local GKIs is severely handicapped by such intergovernmental conflicts. This is only one example, of course, of the ruinous conflicts between the stakeholders.

The Russian state, and in particular GKI, seems to be quite willing to give up control over enterprises. All the evidence indicates that GKI is more interested in privatization than in management. However, GKI does appear to be also interested in representing the interests of a particular stakeholder, namely the half of the population that is not directly employed in state enterprises. This "silent majority" is likely to get nothing out of either worker ownership or nomenklatura privatization. It also, surprisingly, does not have an effective lobby in the Parliament. Championing the silent majority has two advantages. First, it assures a more fair privatization, and hence avoids a subsequent social explosion when it turns out that some people get nothing. Second, allocating shares to the public has the benefit of opening up state firms to outside investors, and hence creating the conditions for effective governance in the future as shares are sold to more efficient investors. From both the equity and the efficiency viewpoint, championing the public is a very wise privatization strategy. Needless to say, the workers and the managers view the allocation of shares to the public as a redistribution from themselves.

Summary

The situation in Russia in 1992 fits well into the general model of multiple owners with overlapping and conflicting control rights. This status quo has two implications for privatization. First, the usual way of resolving disagreements now is to do nothing. Each stakeholder has an effective veto power over any changes. In the context of privatization, this means that any proposal is vetoed, and privatization is delayed. Indeed, some stakeholders, such as many local governments and corporate managers, are quite happy with the status quo since it gives them enormous control rights. There is little hope for extensive privatization until at least some stakeholders get very strong incentives to move away from the status quo.

Second, because the stakeholders have enough effective control to veto any changes, no restructuring can take place. That means no layoffs, no wage restraint, no plant closures, and no management changes until a way of resolving conflicts between stakeholders is found. The local governments, the workers, and the managers can always use their political and economic influence to stop any changes that do not meet their wishes, and their wishes are inconsistent with restructuring. Like privatization, restructuring cannot proceed under the current situation.

To achieve privatization and restructuring, the Russian government must find ways to provide very strong incentives for the existing stakeholders to move to a governance structure that is consistent with fast privatization and restructuring. This objective suggests a two-pronged privatization strategy incorporated into the government's program. First, enterprises should be commercialized or corporatized so that they are separated from the government and their formal governance structure becomes more clearly established. Second, stakeholders should receive strong command and financial incentives, in the form of shares and privatization proceeds, both to preserve the assets of the corporations today and to accede to privatization. Some steps in this direction have already entered the government's program, others are still debated. It makes sense, therefore, to lay out the issues behind this high-pressure approach to privatization.

The Government's Approach to Privatization

Corporatization

In the last two years, many control rights over the assets of state enterprises have been transferred to their managers. In many cases, these managers enjoy their new power and independence, and are in no rush to privatize. When they do consider privatization, it often is spontaneous privatization that completely entrenches them at the helm. In addition, political pressures have led to a transfer of control over privatization of many enterprises to the local governments. Many of the local administrators view this control as the right to manage the state enterprises rather than privatize them. Today, Russia is in grave danger that firms will move toward local administrative control rather than private ownership.

The first essential step to prevent this is mandatory commercialization (or corporatization) of all the enterprises. Corporatization has been introduced into the government privatization program, and mandated by a Yeltsin decree in early July 1992. According to the decree, all large state enterprises should be converted into joint stock companies with publicly traded shares and boards of directors. Initially, all the shares will be held by GKI (or State Property Funds), but over time as the privatization process unfolds, they will be given away or sold to the various stakeholders and investors. The board of directors would initially consist of the representatives of GKI, the managers, the representatives of the workers, bankers, and perhaps others involved with the corporation. After privatization, it would be elected by shareholders as in any private company. The idea is to make the state companies resemble shareholder-owned companies from the start, even if the principal shareholder temporarily remains the state.

Immediate corporatization accomplishes some of the goals of organizing corporate governance and resolving conflicts before privatization. To begin with, it creates boards of directors charged with fiduciary responsibility to maximize the wealth of the shareholders. These boards will serve several functions. First, because of directors' liability, directors will at the least try to prevent the blatant theft of assets by the managers. In some cases, directors will even provide more stringent checks on the management. In contrast to spontaneous privatization, boards of directors institutionalize the possibility of replacing the managers and thereby prevent complete entrenchment. Second, boards become a formal mechanism whereby the relevant stakeholders can exchange information and views. The workers' representatives will both be informed about the affairs of the companies and have the opportunity to formally express their positions. When they can do that, they are less likely to resolve conflicts through strikes. Finally, and perhaps most importantly, boards formalize the fact that shareholders—not the workers or the local governments—own companies and therefore have the formal right to run them. Disputes are resolved by votes on the board rather than by other means. The hope is that this approach will also reduce the destructive competition for rents.

Corporatization also creates tradable shares in the companies, and hence outside shareholders. Initially, the shares will be owned by GKI, which will reinforce the central government's ownership claim. As we discuss below, some shares will immediately be allocated to the workers and the managers, which will clarify their ownership claims as well, and provide them with some incentives to increase the value of the company. Other shares will be sold over time, which will create outside shareholders with value-maximizing objectives. Perhaps even better, the stage is set for GKI to sell control of some of these companies through a sale of controlling blocks of shares. By creating a potential market in the shares of state companies, corporatization moves companies a step closer toward privatization.

But perhaps the greatest potential benefit of corporatization is that it begins the process of separation of enterprises from the state, and therefore from unlimited state credits. The enterprise becomes an independent entity, rather than an integral part of some government agency. As a consequence, it becomes possible to treat it as an independent entity and perhaps even to restrict its credit. In fact, first Deputy Prime Minister Shumeiko has argued for mandatory corporatization for precisely these reasons.

Initially, the idea of corporatization was not received well by the ministries and the managers, since they viewed it as a first step toward taking away their control. Through sheer populist luck, however, the government managed to create at least a partial consensus in favor of corporatization. The government argued that corporatization is necessary to give shares to the enterprise workers and even more importantly to sell shares in the mass privatization program. By pressing these populist arguments for corporatization, the government made it an inevitable part of the privatization program. The government's case was helped by Shumeiko, who sees corporatization as a way to harden the budget constraints on firms.

The Workers

To avoid massive resistance to privatization, the government must pay off the workers. It is important to give workers stakes in their companies to make them feel like owners right away, but also to provide them with strong incentives to actually want to see privatization accomplished. At the same time, GKI must deal with a legitimate and important concern that worker control is inconsistent with efficient corporate restructuring. The privatization program is a significant compromise, in that it gives the workers substantial ownership and returns from privatization without giving them control.

Specifically, the privatization program provides for three alternative benefit packages for the workers. The first alternative gives workers 25 percent of the shares of the state companies they work for, up to a certain ruble limit. Initially, these shares will be nonvoting and will also pay a fairly high dividend. The idea behind making shares nonvoting at the beginning is to prevent worker control before firms are privatized. The law allows workers to trade shares from the start. The idea is in part to enable the workers who want cash to benefit from this transfer immediately, and in part to limit the eventual voting power of the workers. The 25 percent grant of shares gives the workers something regardless of whether privatization is accomplished. To give workers an extra incentive to favor privatization, the law provides them with further benefits. The workers get 10 percent of the government's privatization proceeds. They also get the option to buy 10 percent of the shares of privatized companies at a 30 percent discount to book value, which in most cases is a trivial fraction of true value. Importantly, getting anything out of these programs requires that the government's stake fall below 50 percent. This hopefully will provide enough of a privatization sweetener in addition to the straight giveaway to the workers.

The second alternative might be even more attractive to the workers and the managers in smaller enterprises. The program allows these workers and managers to buy 51 percent of the voting shares of their firms at a discount and with deferred payments as long as workers buy these shares as individuals and as long as the enterprise corporatizes. The remaining shares can be sold to the workers as well, but they now have to compete with the potential outside investors and the public. This MBO option might be particularly attractive to the managers since it would typically enable them to retain control. Indeed, the MBO option was introduced into the program partly to placate the management lobby in the Parliament. At the same time, these MBOs might be too expensive in the ultra-large and capital-intensive companies, and therefore the first option would be chosen. However, so far the second alternative has proven the most popular among all the firms that have submitted privatization plans.

Some managers do not like the MBO option since it does not explicitly allow them to buy a large stake in their company at attractive terms. For this reason, the management lobby campaigned for and obtained an third "worker benefits" option, which would enable the workers and the managers each to buy 20 percent of the company shares at book value. This option is restricted to small and medium-size companies, since the Parliament has correctly identified it as a recipe for creating multimillionaire managers. Even so, a manager of a company with 50 million rubles of book value would, for 10 million rubles that he can borrow from the bank, possibly get something worth 50 or 100 million rubles, since book values are artificially low. This option recognizes very explicitly the extraordinary power of the managers, and their ability to influence the Parliament to transfer resources to themselves.

The three alternatives show the extraordinary generosity of the Russian program toward the workers and the managers—not out of the goodness of the reformers' hearts but out of the recognition of the political reality. Yet such generosity is the only hope of getting the workers and the managers to hop on the privatization bandwagon. Luckily, the government program recognizes this reality rather than worrying excessively about the fairness of the program.

Local Governments

In the former Soviet Union, tensions between governments are not just restricted to those between the former Soviet republics, or those between local governments in Russia and the central Russian government. Tensions also exist between city and oblast governments, oblast and central Russian, and many other layers. In particular, Russia on its territory has several ethnic republics that are laying claim to the property on their territories and threatening to declare independence from Russia if these claims are not respected. In this section, we use the term "local governments" generically, and focus on their relationship with the Russian center.

The strategy toward local governments is to coopt them into supporting privatization and relinquishing their control rights over firms. Given that their claims are often as strong as those of the workers, they will not be cheap to convince. At the same time, they should not be given shares, no matter when these shares become voting, since this strategy makes them large shareholders with a substantial interest in active control. While workers' shares are dispersed, local government shares are concentrated. In many cases, local governments would use their ownership rights to derail privatization and to continue managing the state firms. For this reason, the only feasible way to pay off local governments is by giving them privatization proceeds rather than shares. Fortunately, the Russian privatization program recognizes this and is in fact extremely generous to the local

governments. It gives them both a chunk of the privatization proceeds and a role in privatization, but not shares.

The program divides firms into those under federal, oblast
(or republican), and municipal jurisdiction. Having clas-
sified firms, the Russian program gives oblasts and munici-
palities the responsibility to privatize the enterprises under
their respective jurisdictions, and assigns to the Russian
government the right to privatize the federal ones. It is not
clear who retains ownership in the meantime. Not surprisingly, the question of how many management rights the
local governments actually have has become the most important point of disagreement between them and the center.
The center wants to keep management to a minimum, while
many localities are more interested in management than in
privatization.

The law gives local governments several privatization techniques to choose from, including auctions and competitions.
The latter allow sales based on criteria other than price. The
book value is used as the reserve in these auctions and
competitions. The law also specifies ways of dividing privatization revenue between the federal, oblast, and local
governments. The principal objective of this division is to
prevent conflict in the allocation of firms between levels,
which would arise if the split of privatization revenues
varied greatly depending on who privatized the firm. One
important source of tension in the choice of privatization
techniques has been the insistence of some local governments that they be able to exclude nonresidents from par-

ticipating in auctions for small firms. This preference is driven mostly by the desire to keep auctions thin and so to collect more bribes. While this conflict has not been resolved, the center has been caving in to this pressure from local governments. Whatever the final outcome, giving the local governments a substantial financial incentive to privatize has been the cornerstone of the Russian privatization program.

This decentralized approach to privatization has several advantages. First, it provides local governments with substantial financial incentives to privatize. It also greatly reduces the burden on the central government of finding some privatization arrangements for a large number of enterprises. Since the managers and the workers are likely to get along with the local governments better than they do with the center, they are more likely to find an acceptable solution. Last but not least, the transfer of control over privatization of some firms to the local governments eradicates the role of the ministries in these privatizations virtually completely.

The greatest difficulty with privatization from below is that local governments may simply refuse to privatize and try instead to keep control over firms. After all, the bureaucrats in the local governments get bribes and presents only as long as they keep control over firms. In fact, many local governments have expressed a clear view that they will privatize sometime in the future, but in the meantime have to manage the firms for the benefit of the local populations.

If privatizations in some areas become successful, even the recalcitrant local governments might see the benefits of privatization in the regions that have moved fast, and so feel compelled to follow suit. Competition between regions for foreign investment and for domestic funds might also accelerate privatization. Yet probably the strongest pressure toward privatization might be the desire of the workers and the populations of these areas to get their cut, which will force many of the local governments to privatize so as to satisfy their voters.

A second problem with privatization from below is corruption. While the coffers of the local government benefit from privatization, the pockets of the bureaucrats do not. Pushing privatization down to the local level will create tremendous corruption problems, as the local bureaucrats try to get a cut. This problem is rendered much worse by the fact that the law allows the local governments to use criteria other than price for privatization. Why not, then, sell a firm cheap in exchange for a promise to build a park in the city, or procure food for the town, plus a bribe? In fact, it is often in the interest of the local governments to choose privatization schemes that commit firms to do things for localities, rather than maximize privatization revenue. To some extent, this problem is smaller when localities keep a lion's share of privatization proceeds. Even then, the potential for corruption is truly enormous.

While local control spells corruption everywhere in the world, some steps can be taken to reduce this problem. Most importantly, nonprice methods of allocating firms should be restricted where possible, and auctions (including auctions where each buyer must meet certain terms) should be used instead. Auctions reduce corruption relative to more discretionary forms of sale. Second, the government should require the maximum publicity about firms that are being privatized. Some transparency will prevent the blowup of the privatization process as corruption becomes exposed.

All things considered, putting more pressure on the local governments to privatize is highly desirable. Starving the local government budgets by not allocating funds from the center might provide them with a strong incentive to try to raise money, including by means of privatization. In addition, the pressure from the workers is likely to be extremely important, since workers of state enterprises represent many of the voters in the local elections. For this reason as well, generosity toward workers in accomplished privatizations is desirable.

Managers

Enterprise managers can easily sabotage privatization by refusing to cooperate with either the buyers or the government, and their claims are therefore the most important to respect. Most managers have considerable control over assets now, and will retain most of it no matter what form privatization takes. The Russian government's privatization program recognizes the power of the managers and gives them two very substantial benefits. First, as already discussed, many of the worker benefits are really managers' benefits. Particularly in the MBO alternative and the 20 percent at book value alternative, managers will be able to obtain substantial ownership stakes in their companies at very low prices *and* retain virtually complete control. Many of them would become millionaires immediately. Some would become even richer by subsequently selling stakes in their companies to foreign investors. Any manager in Russia today can use the program to become rich and remain in control.

In addition, the program gives the managers the right to prepare a privatization plan for their company. Even if they decide not to do an MBO or buy a very large stake, they can still essentially decide whether to have a foreign investor, a large domestic investor, or simply dissipate shares between many small investors. In addition, the managers can set many of the terms that would be used in the sale of a large (or controlling) block in the company. Effectively, the managers can veto most privatization solutions that are not acceptable to them. In this, the Russian privatization program imitates the Czechoslovakian experience, in which enterprise managers were successfully enticed to cooperate in privatization.

While the Russian privatization program is extremely generous to the managers, and many of them will undoubtedly take up the government on its offer and privatize, some managers are likely to resist. First, the managers of basically unsound companies would much prefer staying on state subsidies to privatization, since these companies can probably never make money. These managers would also favor the holding companies and other cross-subsidization arrangements. The privatization program has not really figured out what to do with these companies, particularly how to restructure them. Secondly, the managers of the very rich companies would under the current terms have a hard time buying them, and so might prefer to remain in charge without privatization. For example, managers in the oil industry can now buy foreign know-how and assure themselves attractive consumption patterns without privatization. They will not be in a hurry to privatize and give up control. It is not clear how the government at this point can force them to privatize. Despite these reservations, there is hope that many firms will indeed use the benefits to start the privatization process.

Branch Ministries

The one stakeholder to whom the Russian privatization program does not give a lot of benefits is the branch ministries. The workers, the managers who want to privatize, and the local governments seem to be united in trying to diminish ministerial control, since it directly conflicts with their rights. In fact, the privatization proposal that the ministries seem to support is that of holding companies organized by the ministries that hold the shares of state enterprises rather than give or sell them to the workers, the managers, or the public. Clearly, those workers and managers who want to profit from privatization do not want this alternative, although the managers who want the status quo to be preserved surely like it. Moreover, from the long-run efficiency viewpoint, any control by the ministries is bad for the simple reason that the ministries are a substitute for market transactions and giving them a role would reduce the role of the market. In particular, privatization is strictly against the interests of the ministries. If the ministries get control rights through the holding companies, they would use them not to facilitate the allocation of firms into the private sector, but rather to entrench themselves.

Of course, as we have already mentioned, the ministries still have some control over enterprises and voting power in the government. Excluding them completely from the privatization process will be costly. The current privatization recognizes this and concedes to the ministries in two important respects. First, they will be able to review and perhaps reject privatization plans for large federal enterprises. It is not entirely obvious what legal status these reviews will have. In particular, the government has so far resisted giving a large role in its privatization program to sectoral privatization plans that will be developed by the ministries. Second, some of the shares will probably be distributed along the vertical production chain and some holding companies will be formed, as the ministries like. It is not clear how common or dangerous these holding companies will be, although the initial indications are very troublesome. The ministerial version, whereby shares are allocated administratively and held by the central office, is frightening. The less obtrusive version is just some exchange of shares between enterprises, without the centralized allocation mechanisms. The form of holdings will undoubtedly determine the shape of privatization of the very large enterprises. The ministries will get something, but hopefully not enough to stop privatization from going ahead.

The Public

Perhaps the most important stakeholder in the Russian privatization program is the public, which includes several important categories of people who do not benefit from the free handouts or subsidized sales of shares. The public includes pensioners, students, invalids, and other citizens supported directly by the state budget. The public also includes doctors, teachers, professors, and others who do not work at firms that will be privatized. Perhaps most importantly, the public includes the army that is very hungry and very angry. Altogether, the public is roughly half of the adult population.

The public has some political power, and wants to benefit from privatization like everyone else. It is not aggressively represented in the Parliament, but it is ready to demonstrate in the streets, and, in the case of the military, offers a potentially much greater threat to the government. Like every other privatizing country, Russia must give something to the public for privatization to succeed. Indeed, mass privatization is the central feature of the government privatization program.

The program incorporates a voucher scheme similar to that used in Czechoslovakia. In this scheme, members of the public will be given individual vouchers that will give them claims to shares of privatizing companies. Of the shares not going to workers on preferential terms, 80–90 percent will be sold for vouchers. Individuals will be able to sell these vouchers for cash, to turn them over to mutual funds that will use them to buy shares of privatizing companies, or even to use the vouchers to bid for shares directly. Shares will be sold for vouchers, and individuals and mutual funds can bid.

While the government is very sympathetic to the idea of having private mutual funds to collect or buy vouchers, it is resisting the idea of Polish-style state-sponsored mutual funds, which might prove difficult to separate from the government in Russia. As a result, such funds might not be able to solve the soft–budget constraint problem, which is one of the fundamental deterrents to the restructuring of the Russian enterprises. Nonetheless, as in Czechoslovakia, mutual funds will play a critical role in pooling the population's vouchers and using them to buy enterprise shares.

Perhaps the most interesting aspect of the voucher program in Russia is its importance in getting the program through in its current form. Vouchers played a role in assuring the acceptance of corporatization, since the enterprises needed to offer shares to the public in exchange for vouchers. Vouchers helped prevent universal holding companies, since these again are incompatible with selling shares to the public. Finally, vouchers played an important role in stopping even more extreme giveaways to the workers and the managers—such as giving them their companies outright—again because something had to be left for the public. In the end, the populist aspect of vouchers may have saved the Russian privatization program.

Summary

In this section we have outlined some strategies of the Russian privatization program. These strategies invite the workers and the local governments to give up their control rights, and allocate these rights to the managers and the new investors. But even if all the steps described in this section are taken, conflicts over privatization and restructuring will remain. Nonetheless, the legislation should continue to move in the direction of providing compensation for the stakeholders in return for cooperating in privatization.

The Future of Privatization

In this section, we will consider both what can go right with the Russian privatization and what can go wrong. We will try to anticipate some of the likely successes, but also focus on the many obstacles that still exist. Overall, while the passage of the program through the Parliament creates some grounds for optimism, many things can still go wrong.

The Likely Successes

In many cases, privatization in Russia is likely to proceed quite rapidly. Perhaps the greatest hope is that privatization of small shops, automobiles, and other relatively small businesses will begin very fast, *particularly when local governments are receptive.* In Nizhni Novgorod, St. Petersburg, Moscow, and a few other cities, such small-scale privatization has already begun. Where auctions have been used, the prices received have been fantastic. The initial prices in these auctions by law are equal to the book value of assets. Yet eventual prices are often 50 to 100 times higher! For example, in St. Petersburg small businesses in nice locations with book value assets of under 100,000 rubles have fetched prices over 20 million rubles. In Moscow, shops are being sold to their workers at fixed (very low) prices, since Moscow has been allowed by Yeltsin's decree to follow its own privatization policy. Yet even in Moscow, such small-scale privatization is well under way. What seems to be essential to all these stories is that the local government is interested in privatization: more on this later.

The privatization of small-scale enterprises, those with up to a few hundred workers, has already begun as well and is likely to accelerate now that the privatization program has been passed by the Parliament. Many of these firms have been privatized spontaneously, through legal or illegal worker management buyouts. Others are now leased and will be bought out by the workers and the managers. Yet others will simply choose either option 2 or option 3 of workers' benefits and go through a buyout. The prices in these buyouts have been and are going to be ridiculously low, since book values of the Russian enterprises are trivial even compared to their low profitability. At these prices, credit and repayment will not be difficult. As a result, enterprises that have any hope of survival in the marketplace, and that have even moderately aggressive managers, will probably move to privatize in the near future. Those that have some earnings potential but not energetic managers will probably soon see offers from outsiders to do a buyout with some outside participation. Again, assuming that local governments are cooperating, we can be optimistic that medium-scale privatization will proceed.

With very large enterprises, buyouts and acquisitions of large blocks at book value may turn out to be more expensive but are still likely to be possible. Consider the following example. A typical large industrial firm in Russia has roughly 20,000 rubles of fixed capital per worker at book value; in most cases this amount is below 40,000 rubles anyway. To gain control, workers need to buy out half of that, or 10,000 to 20,000 rubles per worker. The voucher program gives each citizen 10,000 rubles. This means that a worker from a family with three other members has roughly 30,000 to 40,000 rubles of purchasing power at his (or her) disposal. As long as the worker-management buyouts are at prices below twice the book value, which they are, such a worker will have enough in vouchers to buy his or her shares. In most cases, then, worker-management buyouts will not be prohibitive if they are desired.

Selling blocks of shares in large enterprises will be more difficult if the managers and workers are not interested. Such enterprises either will need outside investors—who most likely will be foreigners—or will simply go through voucher privatization and not have a large blockholder. Foreign investment in Russia is likely to be at best moderate in the near future. Part of the problem is still a tremendous lack of clarity in laws and authority. Another part is that many managers will insist on retaining control, which they essentially can insist on under the government's program. However, many foreigners might not be interested in Russian companies without getting control. While there are certain to be some demonstration projects involving foreign investors, the government should not count on FDI as an important part of the program. More likely, control of the large enterprises will be dispersed, or else their privatization will be delayed until the future, with the managers retaining interim control.

The Likely Dangers

The passage of the privatization program without a radical change has removed one potential stumbling block in the Russian privatization. Nonetheless, many other problems remain. This subsection focuses on four potentially important problems. This list, of course, is not exclusive, and many other mishaps can derail privatization in Russia.

One extremely important constraint is the limitation on GKI resources. GKI has to prepare a great number of regulations to provide guidance to enterprises in corporation, design of privatization plans, finding outside investors, share sales, and other steps. GKI needs to train its staff in implementing the privatization program without delays. GKI needs to design and implement the voucher program, which by itself is a massive undertaking. Finally, GKI actually needs to oversee and approve privatizations, including selling shares to the public. The purely administrative constraints that GKI faces might become a significant obstacle in allowing privatization to go forward.

A second potentially dangerous constraint is the conflict between GKI and the property funds. The privatization law of 1991 has created two parallel institutions responsible for selling state enterprises. One is GKI, which is accountable to the government. The other is the property funds, which nominally hold the property and are accountable to the Parliament. Indeed, the Parliament has created the two-tiered structure precisely to keep some control over privatization in the legislative branch rather than handing it over completely to the executive branch. This political maneuver, however, creates significant difficulties that the Russian privatization will have to overcome. In many locations, property funds have not yet been created, or else are very passive. In other locations, such as Moscow and St. Petersburg, they have been very active and have blocked privatization projects. There is no doubt that they will often insist on particular strategies that will come in conflict with the government's program or the objectives of GKI. There is considerable danger that the tensions between the two agencies will slow down privatization in some regions.

A third very important constraint concerns very large companies and has been mentioned in passing before. Specifically, there is a significant number of managers of large state enterprises, supported by influential figures in the Russian government, who want to put shares of corporatized state companies into holding companies organized by the ministries. There is little doubt that such a strategy will completely stop privatization and restructuring of these enterprises. Its twofold goals are to give the ministries something to do (which is why the ministries like it) and to keep credit flowing to state enterprises (which is why the managers like it). If holding companies of the ministerial variety become important, one can forget about privatization of very large companies in Russia. The best weapon against these holdings that GKI has is of course the voucher scheme.

But perhaps the greatest danger to privatization in Russia is the local governments, which as we have mentioned often want to manage the enterprises rather than privatize them. It is fair to say that the center does not have any strong weapons to force these local governments to privatize. It is hoped that budgetary pressures will prevail on some governments, particularly after they see the high prices obtained in auctions in St. Petersburg and Nizhni Novgorod. Even stronger pressure might come from the workers who want their free shares or subsidized buyouts. Yet further pressure will come from the public that will have the vouchers. Whether all these pressures will turn out to be sufficient to induce the local governments to privatize remains to be seen, however.

Overall, then, there are likely to be some bright and some less bright spots in Russian privatization in the near future. The bright spots are going to be small and medium-scale privatizations in the areas with progressive governments. The less bright spots will be the more reactionary local governments and large-scale privatization. Perhaps the key results for GKI to hope for is to build up the momentum and the enthusiasm for privatization, so that it becomes an irreversible process.

Russian Privatization and the Monopoly Problem

An important special problem confronting the Russian reform is the prevalence of firms with a very large market share in many industries. The socialist planners practiced specialization to an enormous extent, with the result that many industries consist of monopolies or at best duopolies. The problem is made worse by the fact that trade in intermediate goods and wholesale trade are still controlled by the state, and the state supply network is in many instances not functioning. As a result, even where two potential suppliers of a given input or product exist, only one can actually deliver the goods to the buyers through the state supply network.

These problems have stimulated some observers to call for a breakup of state monopolies prior to privatization (Tirole 1991). The idea is to create potential competition while the state still has some control over these enterprises, so that their ability to raise prices after privatization is at least limited by competition. The fact that many state monopolies in Russia have plants in many locations might make such breakups easier.

We agree that such preprivatization restructuring is a desirable objective. However, given the political context of Russian privatization, particularly the overwhelming control of the enterprise managers over the privatization process, a mandatory breakup of state monopolies prior to privatization is completely unrealistic. No state agency conceivably has the power to break up large state monopolies. Using a more decentralized approach, the Russian privatization program has allowed divisions of large state enterprises to break off and privatize separately, but with virtually no exceptions top enterprise managers have prevented this from happening. The gas monopoly, for example, successfully resisted the withdrawal of collective farms from its control, let alone gas properties.

If state monopolies cannot be broken up, should they be privatized at all? The traditional fear of privatizing monopolies is that they will raise prices after privatization. The argument is that controlling monopoly prices is easier under state ownership, when presumably the managers do not have a strong incentive to maximize profits and the government has some control rights, then under private ownership, when the managers have stronger profit-maximizing incentives and the government has even less power.

We are skeptical about this argument. First, Russian enterprise managers have a great deal of price-setting authority already, and are probably charging monopoly prices to the extent they can despite state ownership. What limits such prices today is not state ownership but rather interest in preserving long-term relationships with buyers, as well as in some cases lack of demand for the low-quality products produced by the state monopolies. It is not clear that managerial control will increase all that much after privatization. Second, price regulation is not particularly effective either before or after privatization. In Russia even more than in the West, the regulators have been completely captured by the state enterprises, which in many cases are paying the regulators' operating costs, and are likely to remain captured after privatization. If anything, regulation might become more effective after privatization, when the monopolies are at least partly separated from their regulators. Thus we do not see monopoly pricing as an argument against privatization.

Moreover, we do not see monopoly pricing to be the greatest danger of state monopolies. By far the greater danger is the enormous subsidies flowing to these firms from the State Bank designed to enable them not to restructure, and to maintain employment and output. These subsidies are the main reason for a high inflation in Russia, and are by far the greatest obstacle to comprehensive reform.

To be sure, in most cases these subsidies to monopolies will continue after privatization just as they did before. Monopolies—public or private—because of their size and the lack of substitutes for their products, have a unique power to blackmail the government to provide them with cash injections. For this reason, privatization of monopolies might in most cases be ineffective in the short run, since restructuring of monopolies is incompatible with the government's objectives. Nonetheless, in at least some cases, the privatized monopolies will try to cut costs and restructure—a strategy they are less likely to pursue under public ownership. These few cases will *in the short run* be the main reason for privatizing public monopolies. In the longer run, of course, as the government in Russia becomes stronger and more able to resist demands for subsidies, even more private monopolies will restructure.

These arguments lead us to believe that state monopolies in Russia should be privatized together with other public enterprises. We are not optimistic that in the short run many of these monopolies will restructure. Nonetheless, on balance, there will be more restructuring under private than under public control.

The arguments we have made, particularly the ability of state monopolies to extract subsidies from the government, have not escaped their managers. The irony of Russian privatization is that, far from breaking up state monopolies prior to privatization, the pressure is on the government to *consolidate* them. Specifically, the Parliament, the managerial lobby, and the members of the government who respond to this lobby's demands want to create holding companies that would control the assets of separate enterprises in an industry. Once the holding company is created, presumably through an exchange of controlling blocks of shares between member enterprises, the remaining shares are sold to the public in "privatization." The proposed holding companies in Russia are similar to trusts in the turn-of-the-century United States, except that government control is usually preserved.

There are obviously two reasons for creating these holding companies. The first is to raise prices collectively and to prevent competition. In this respect, holding companies are just like the trusts. The second and far more dangerous reason is to present a unified threat to the government of cutting employment and production, and hence to extract greater subsidies. In fact, the current industry associations in Russia, which hope to become the governing bodies of holding companies, openly announce that their greatest accomplishment is the extraction of subsidies from the state.

This brings us to what we consider by far the most important element of a plausible antimonopoly policy in Russia, namely to stop the formation of holding companies, or at of such companies based on horizontal ties. In the regime of poor supply assurance, one could perhaps argue for vertical integration as a basis for holding companies. But horizontal consolidations, which many advocates of holdings have in mind, are the surest way to block the restructuring of state enterprises in the foreseeable future. Thus there is room for an active antimonopoly policy in Russia—not to break up the existing monopolies, but to hold off the creation of new ones.

Conclusion

In this chapter we described privatization as a redistribution of existing control rights over company assets between its stakeholders. To get the stakeholders to agree to this redistribution, they need to be compensated in terms of dividends and privatization proceeds. We have discussed the ways in which the Russian privatization program incorporates schemes of providing this compensation to the workers, the managers, and the local governments, the three principal forces that might oppose privatization. While these schemes will not stop all the resistance to privatization, they might well reduce it.

It is impossible to tell how fast privatization will proceed in Russia. Many bureaucrats, politicians, and managers oppose it, and have enough political clout to slow it down. Even after privatization, restructuring may not come. The managers and the workers of privatized enterprises will surely try to use their influence with the government to get subsidies, and, unless the government tightens its monetary policy, in many cases they will receive what they ask for. Unemployment might also prove to be politically unpalatable, which will slow down restructuring a great deal. These problems suggest that Russia, even more than other Eastern European countries, will feel the pain of restructuring even if privatization succeeds. Yet to get to the point where restructuring is seriously contemplated, Russia needs to be privatized. It is therefore essential to push for this, and to grease the wheels when they are slow-turning.

4　Payments Arrangements among the Republics

Until recently, the United States and most of Western Europe strongly supported the existence of a united Soviet Union and actively discouraged a breakup. But the breakup has now occurred; the new Commonwealth structure seemed a solution for a while, but that is no longer the case. Ukraine has already split off and is running a hyperinflation on its "coupons." At the other extreme Estonia has created its own money on a hard basis, using a currency board scheme, i.e., a currency fully backed, at least at the margin, by foreign exchange and a fixed exchange rate. The Russian government planned a firm decision on a ruble area by January 1993. Countries would have to choose whether to be part of the ruble zone and subordinate themselves to Moscow or else go off on their own.

The introduction of national currencies has been slow because of the sheer physical lack of new money and because of a substantial lack of familiarity with financial issues outside Moscow. But it presumably remains a strong point on the political agenda of the new nationalism. Thus, if intense

Written by Rudiger Dornbusch.

disunion emerges, with new frontiers and new monies, an Eastern Payments Mechanism (EPM) might help avoid unnecessary trade collapse.

There are two reform options: one is that each country move immediately to convertibility and the other is to develop a mechanism such as the European Payments Union of the postwar period. Full and early convertibility is the preferred answer of economists, officials in the West, and the IMF. But politicians in the former Soviet Union are more skeptical of reform and are surely reluctant to go immediately all the way. They fear the loss of economic control, just as Europe did in the postwar period. But absent convertibility, as each country seeks control of its foreign exchange outlays or of its underpriced and hence scarce exports by itself and without thinking about the system-wide consequences of its policies, risks of a trade collapse increase sharply. The perception of a dollar shortage, with everybody acting as if they were illiquid, inevitably engenders trade collapse.

The payments mechanism proposed here is not a new idea by any means, nor is it a panacea. (See, for example, van Brabant 1991; Havrylyshyn and Williamson 1991; Bofinger 1990, 1991a, 1991b; Gros 1991; Kenen 1991; and Gros, Pisany-Ferry, and Sapir 1992.) By itself, without complementary reforms, it will do virtually nothing to improve the outlook. But as part of a reform effort, and if full convertibility is not acceptable immediately and for all, it can help maintain trade among the republics and revive some of the trade with Eastern Europe that vanished needlessly. Trade between Cuba and the USSR was high almost exclusively for political reasons, but trade among the members of the former Soviet Union certainly has an important geographic motivation. There is no presumption that most of this trade should go overboard in favor of a dominant new trade orientation toward industrialized countries. Of course, each member of the former Soviet bloc is likely to trade more with the West than before, and most may wind up trading less with Moscow (Collins and Rodrik 1991; Hamilton and Winters 1992). But in the meantime, before new trading patterns emerge, little purpose is served in risking a wholesale destruction of production merely because the lack of a payments mechanism stands in the way of continuing trade.

Among the sharpest critics of any payments scheme, in part out of ignorance, are former Eastern European partners in the COMECON who have moved to convertibility and a Western-oriented trade. Poland, Hungary, and Czechoslovakia have more than made up their trade losses with increased exports to the West. But their partners in the East are left stranded. And even the more successful Eastern European economies could do far better by continuing trade relations with the former partners.

The Problem and the Risks

The breakdown of internal trade among various republics of the Soviet Union is happening for a number of reasons. Each reason is enough to disrupt trade; together the effect is likely to be devastating. Just what can happen is made clear by what has happened to COMECON trade.

Eastern Europe, in the transition from Communist rule, is already witnessing a massive fall of trade within the region. It might be argued that some trade should disappear, being based on plans rather than markets, but it is equally clear that *some* of the trade made perfect sense—Polish potatoes for Russian gas—but fell victim to some malfunction. Trade between the former Soviet Union and members of COMECON has fallen by more than 50 percent in the period 1988–1991.

The extraordinary degree of specialization of the republics makes each of the economies far more vulnerable to trade disruption than would be the case in the West. Massive reliance on scale economies led to the creation of firms so large that less than a handful supplied the entire Soviet

Table 4.1
Trade Dependence

	Exports[1]		Trade Balance[2]	
	Interrepublican	Total	Interrepublican	Total
Russia	18.0	36.8	28.5	41.3
Ukraine	39.1	45.8	−3.9	−5.4
Belarus	69.6	76.1	−0.2	−2.5
Kazakhstan	30.9	33.8	−1.1	−7.7
Uzbekistan	43.2	50.5	0.1	−4.4

1. Percent of net material product (NMP).
2. In million rubles at world market prices.
Source: IMF et al. (1991).

market in a particular commodity group. Intraunion trade accounts for 71 percent of the republics' total trade, on average, far more than trade among Canadian provinces or intra-European trade in the case of the European Community (IMF 1992).

Belarus offers perhaps the most extreme example of the degree of interdependence: more than three-quarters of the country's NMP is represented by foreign trade, 70 percent of which is with other republics.

The specialization brings with it the potential for an extraordinary chain reaction: with so much specialization, if deliveries fail anywhere, the entire chain of production in an industry can break down. The failure to have these final goods on hand for trading further widens the inability to import and produce.

The lack of a price system, to some extent even now in Russia but much more so in other republics, makes it extremely unattractive to trade goods for rubles; barter is more attractive because at least there is a counterpart in goods received. But barter is hard to arrange and there is now a proliferation of competing authorities in different republics that might assert their claim to certain goods. This threat alone is cutting off trade.

The lack of an effective payments system further aggravates the situation. If payments take months to clear, as is the case today, who wants to be a creditor in a period of hyperinflation?

Nationalism is emerging as an issue. From the republican perspective, sending goods to Moscow is being questioned, certainly if they are exchanged for rubles. Moscow is looking skeptically at delivering underpriced goods like oil or other tradable goods to the republics, as the opportunity cost of the implied subsidies is becoming crystal clear.

Lack of trust is the newest problem, a luxury that did not exist under central communist rule. With central control and enforcement gone, an institutional vacuum has opened up. If, for seasonal reasons or otherwise, a barter deal involves delays between receipt and shipment of goods, who is to know whether the quid pro quo will actually arrive? Without a guarantee mechanism, fewer trade risks will be taken especially if nobody has any idea who might be responsible or liable for failure to deliver on a contract.

The ruble is no longer an effective medium of exchange for the entire Soviet Union. This situation has arisen in part because of the lack of full internal convertibility (i.e., there is at best a limited price and market system) and in part because of its deteriorating quality as an asset (i.e., the black market purchasing power of the ruble in terms of goods and foreign exchange is vanishing). Of course, price liberalization has gone some way toward creating a market, though regulation and administration remain pervasive. But even the limited usefulness of this currency is being put in question by the possibility of imminent monetary reforms that will introduce new monies and freeze or just write off old ones.

With an opening to the West, captive markets for goods are disappearing and alternative sources of supply are growing. Because of a desire to take advantage of the new markets, dollars could assume an entirely special quality because they can allow direct access to *any* good *now*. Rubles, it is feared, will get you nothing now and less later. Given this perception, a dollar shortage might emerge. If this happens, settling interrepublic imbalances in hard currency will seem less unattractive than cutting down on imports to save scarce foreign exchange for trade with the West. Of course, trade restriction is a two-way street; if one country contracts, the other experiences larger imbalances and will have to cut down in turn.

Essentials

An ideal economic system to facilitate trade has the following characteristics: In each country there exists an operating price system, no restrictions on the right to trade, no obstacles to trade such as tariffs, permits, or quotas, a fully convertible (i.e., no exchange control or licenses) and stable currency, and a well-functioning system of trade credit. Such an economy is not in place now in Eastern Europe and there is little prospect of creating it overnight. It is tempting to maintain an uncompromising insistence that reformers go for nothing less than this, but there are few examples in history to encourage that position. To be fair, Czechoslovakia in the aftermath of the Austro-Hungarian empire went far in fulfilling the conditions, but who else did?

Even if some republics managed to implement the complete set of reforms, unless all do their interaction will pose difficulties. Trade problems emerge as much from the best performer, who can exercise choice, as from the worst, who will be led to shore up the external effects of internal mismanagement by increasing degrees of trade restriction. A pessimistic view of the chances of reform, in extent and timing, therefore aims at a system that incorporates countries at various stages of reform where some are far behind others.

Price Reform

Internal price liberalization is the only *absolute* prerequisite to maintain trade because nobody will voluntarily sell below cost. The role previously played by plan and coercion, and now weakly sustained by sheer inertia, has to be augmented by a price system. Without price reform goods will not move, at least not in official hands. In the West, sellers send Christmas cards to buyers. In the former Soviet Union, the cards go to the sellers since, with goods underpriced in terms of rubles, the latter are in command. For goods to move, sellers have to be willing to part with them. Without effective coercion (administration), prices are the only way to accomplish this.

In Russia the reformist Gaidar government must get the credit for pushing price reform quite far. It is clear, too, that they were not politically successful, at least as judged by the fall of the prime minister. Perhaps because they failed to create an ideology to support their measures and create a momentum, perhaps because Russians would rather stand on line, they failed politically. In Ukraine the pendulum is already swinging starkly in the opposite direction. Here control rather than the market is thought to be the best way of handling the economic crisis. In the short run there may, indeed, be more of an appearance of stability. But who doubts that the end of control economies is here and who doubts that Ukraine faces a dramatic disaster?

If a government were unusually able and effective, a gradual and strategic decontrol might be possible. But the cruel fact is that the government is not in a position to administer an ambitious program of staged decontrol. The absence of both *command* and *prices* leaves economic actors without a blueprint on how to keep afloat an immensely specialized economy. Precisely because the economy is so specialized, because scale went hand in hand with command, the vulnerability today is extreme and the need for prices acute. Prices and markets are an effective means to decontrol decisions. In the no-man's land between coercion and a price system with markets and institutions decentralized economies simply cease functioning.

One argument for price controls is their use as a means of maintaining an affordable supply of food to the people. However, postponing price liberalization for food risks major distribution problems, including the threat of unrest as troops help themselves, republics refuse to give up goods, and others have no means but coercion to get access. In the same way, mispricing of raw materials and intermediate goods leads to their hoarding or diversion to world markets with the result that final goods production grinds to a standstill. The extreme degree of specialization at the final goods stage makes this problem particularly threatening.

Recognizing the parallel with Poland is appropriate. (For an account of the Polish experience, see Sachs 1991.) The radical price liberalization in Poland makes one thing certain—nobody is talking about famine. In Poland, unlike in the Soviet Union, goods are available in the shops. Of course, for most people, the perception is that they cannot afford the goods that are there. But even that perception understates the progress. The availability of goods has become a powerful engine in motivating people to work harder, take initiatives, and find ways to earn the incomes that represent the tickets for goods. In the former USSR, Poland's performance is often viewed with horror and portrayed as the one course that is unacceptable. A more mature view is that only in the most optimistic scenario can the Soviet Union make the required adjustments as effectively as was done in Poland.

A Payments System

It is necessary neither that there be a single money nor that the various monies that come into existence be particularly hard. In each country, governments can regulate as they wish who can participate in foreign trade and what incentives or disincentives they might be offered. Even so, some payments system is required. The current arrangements for settling interfirm debts, even within a republic, are cumbersome to the point of being unbelievable. Enormous delays in the settlement of credits have built up mountains of unpaid enterprise debt. It is hard to say what part is simply not paid and what part is unsettled. A modern payments system is not complicated to put in place and the sooner it emerges the sooner credit- and payments-related collapse of production can be forestalled.

Why not go all the way: let the exchange rate settle at whatever level is necessary and let trade flourish? The basic answer is that politicians react viscerally against the notion that a price or an exchange rate should settle at "whatever level necessary to balance demand and supply." Their business is politics and they immediately identify many good reasons (from their perspective) why convertibility should and can be restricted. They fear that the exchange rate will depreciate substantially because all the wrong things will be imported—there are Cadillacs for sale in Russia now—and these imports will depress the exchange rate and thus raise the cost and price of essential imports. Moreover, politicians will recognize that at the outset, reinforced by monetary instability, capital is more likely to leave than come.

Exchange control is a visceral response to a situation that has little political appeal. Of course, in the swing of the pendulum, pervasive intrusion which is associated with controls will also become unpopular, but that is only later. The immediate reaction is against an "equilibrium" exchange rate of 500 rubles to the dollar that makes for pensions of $5 a month and civil service salaries of $40.

The European Payments Union

Western Europe emerged from World War II with price control, demilitarization problems, soft and inconvertible currencies, and massive trade restrictions that were meant to conserve the very scarce foreign exchange. (See Milward 1987; Kaplan and Schleiminger 1989; Yeager 1966; and Patterson 1953.) Bilateral barter trade was the rule. But the efficiency of bilateral balancing quickly became burdensome.

Three problems in particular needed attention. One was the need for some "swing," i.e., for short-term credit lines that would allow countries to avoid the need for strict balancing of bilateral trade each month. Another problem was the inability to use a multilateral offset mechanism that would allow a country to use its net balance with one European country as a means of settling a bilateral deficit with another.

A third problem arose when every country tried to run surpluses in bilateral trade, seeking net dollar balances that could then be used for trade with countries like the US. The strategy used to earn surpluses was, of course, a sure way to lead to trade contraction via restrictions. The Intra-European Payments and Compensation System (IEPS) made some headway in introducing multilateral clearing. But not until the establishment of the EPU was a comprehensive mechanism developed.

The basic provisions of the EPU were as follows:

· The system was operated by the Bank for International Settlements (BIS), an intergovernmental institution created in the interwar years. Once a month the central banks would report their total *net* claims on each member to the BIS. These claims would be calculated on the basis of the declared dollar parity of the respective members. (IMF members were required to maintain bilateral rates consistent with their declared dollar parities.) The BIS as agent of the EPU would undertake multilateral clearing, offsetting surpluses with one country and deficits with another to arrive at the net position. A country would be credited for the total net dollar balance, or debited if there was a total net deficit.

· The extent of credit in the system was determined by quotas and cumulative creditor or debtor positions. Each country would receive a quota based on its "turnover," defined as exports plus imports. This quota would determine the access to credit, according to a system of "tranches."

The financing of imbalances proceeded according to the criterion of *cumulative* imbalances of a member with the Union since the beginning of the EPU. The first 20 percent of the quota could be used without restrictions. But if a country were to build up further imbalances, a portion had to be settled in gold or dollars and only the remainder was financed by credit. The exact share to be settled in hard currency was (with some variation over time) 50 percent. Once a quota was exhausted, the settlement of imbalances had to be made fully in hard currency.

Creditors in turn would receive a portion of their cumulative balances in hard currency and agreed to extend credit for the rest.

· Countries agreed to progressively liberalize trade among the membership.

· The United States politically supported the establishment of the EPU and helped capitalize it. A strong and unified Europe was seen as the strongest defense against Communism.

· The EPU functioned from 1950 until 1958, when most members took their currencies to full current account convertibility. The initial agreement provided for a two-year, renewable operation. Subsequent renewals were for one-year periods. A simple majority of members (as represented by quotas) could ask for dissolution and final settlement.

· The EPU was managed by a board. The board was influential not by any specific power it had but rather on the basis of recommendations that it made when payments problems emerged. And, although difficulties did emerge at the outset, peer pressure proved highly effective in bringing about adjustment.

Table 4.2 gives an impression of persistence and reversals in cumulative creditor positions. Since quotas were set at 15

Table 4.2
Quotas and Cumulative EPU Balances

	Quota	1950	1951	1952
Austria	70	−37.4	−130.6	−108.8
Belg.-Lux.	360	21.8	604.3	761.3
Denmark	195	−38.4	−33.5	−27.3
France	520	212.4	−196.9	−625.7
Germany	500	−356.7	431.4	366.0
Greece	45	−70.8	−186.7	−229.0
Iceland	15	−3.3	−8.5	−12.5
Italy	205	−30.9	195.2	104.9
Netherlands	355	−107.9	−53.1	266.3
Norway	200	−51.1	−70.1	−76.9
Portugal	70	36.8	97.4	66.7
Sweden	260	0	177.2	208.8
Switzerland	250	−12.6	141.9	195.6
Turkey	50	5.3	−98.9	−218.1
UK	1060	433.0	−469.0	−682.2

Source: Patterson (1953).

percent of 1949 turnover, the imbalances were substantial. Where they exceeded quotas special arrangements had to be made.

In looking at the success of the EPU as a mechanism, two questions should be asked. First, how much *multi*lateral clearing was there? Second, how much credit was granted? These are the two ways in which the EPU would operate as a trade-creating facility. The entire history of the EPU can be summarized by the data presented in table 4.3. The total sum of monthly imbalances (double counting) was $46.4 billion. Somewhat less than half was immediately cleared

Table 4.3
An EPU History: 1950–1958 (billion $US)

Total bilateral positions[1]	46.4
Settled by:	
Multilateral compensation	20.0
Compensation through time	12.6
Gold and dollars	10.7
Special settlements	0.5
Credit balance outstanding[2]	2.7

1. Sum of monthly surpluses and deficits.
2. The credit balance in 1958 was settled by special arrangements between net debtors and creditors, primarily France and Germany.
Source: Yeager (1966).

by multilateral offsetting. This fact supports the claim that multilateralism *does* take away the strain of bilateral balancing. About a quarter ($12.6 billion) was settled by credit and subsequent reversal of imbalances. Thus a country would borrow from the union for some time and then run a string of surpluses that would extinguish the debt. Settlement in hard currency amounted to just under a quarter, so clearly there was hard currency discipline in the system. Moreover, hard currency discipline increased substantially in the later stages of the system.

The Relevance of an Eastern Payments Mechanism: Questions and Answers

A payments union today is viewed with great suspicion by almost everyone. Everybody feels that it might just be the vehicle for the other republics to continue or even increase unfair trade. The easiest way to build the case for an Eastern Payments Union is to restate, and answer, the questions and objections that are typically raised. Here are some of the most important questions:

What is the advantage of the mechanism?

Multilateral clearing and limited credit avoids a state of siege on the trade front. It allows fewer restrictions designed to save hard currencies for trade with the outside world.

Even if there is a case for a payments mechanism, why not go all the way to convertibility? In fact, is a payments mechanism not really an obstacle to full reform?

Full convertibility is desirable at the earliest possible stage. In postwar Western Europe it took until 1958, and it is clear in hindsight that the slowest countries were using the convenience of the mechanism to slow down those that could have moved faster. But the EPU also created an important trade zone that might not have arisen if countries had moved individually, made mistakes, and simply rolled back convertibility.

It is essential today to maintain an open internal market in the East. With restraints on competitive exports such as oil and raw materials and limits on imports arising from a super-high shortage of dollars for exchange, the Soviet Union's successor countries would experience a catastrophic decline in their standard of living. A payments union helps build the common market and can evolve increasingly to full convertibility—say in 3 years or 4 years, or even in 2—by simply increasing the portion of imbalances that has to be settled in hard currency. If that portion is 100 percent, the situation corresponds to full convertibility.

Can an EPM be used even when countries have different currencies?

Yes. The point of the mechanism is to use the offsetting of balances so that no hard currency is used for settlement. The credit mechanism (with discipline) is another means to save on foreign exchange.

How can one be sure that a country is not cheated by the system?

The member countries jointly guarantee the credits. It is (barely) conceivable that a country might walk out, but the remaining ones would still be guarantors of the shared balance. Of course, the mechanism also gives group sanction to raise the cost of upsetting the system. And if the West supports the system, then Western sanctions in the form of reduced aid will be an effective way to give the system confidence.

Does a payments mechanism require fixed exchange rates?

By no means. The monthly settlements are done at the average exchange rate of the month.[1] There is no need for that rate to be a constant from one month to the next. The books are kept in dollars so that even if a member experiences hyperinflation, the "real" opportunities and liabilities are unaffected.

What discipline does the system create to cope with large, cumulative deficits?

Hard currency settlement for a fraction of the cumulative imbalance ensures that deficits are not free—they have to be settled in dollars. As countries run out of dollars and reach their quota ceiling, they will have to make adjustments in their exchange rate and/or macroeconomic policies because they now must settle 100 percent in dollars.

After price reform some republics could have large deficits because they import vital goods such as oil. How can the payments union help?

The payments mechanism can only help bring about multilateralism and limited credit. It is not primarily a mechanism for transfers or aid. Countries that import oil will want to set prices at world levels and bring about conservation. Russia may or may not decide to make transfers, but it cannot afford to misprice oil or any other tradable good for very long.

The settlement of imbalances on the basis of *cumulative* imbalances implies that a country that runs a deficit month after month moves quickly into upper tranches of the credit line and has to settle increasingly in hard currency.

How do firms in one country trade with those in another if their currency is inconvertible?

In each member country there will probably be exchange control regulations that will specify the transactions for which firms can make contracts abroad. With a payments union, the set of goods that is liberalized for intraunion trade tends to be wider than what is liberalized for trade with countries outside the union. Firms pay their central bank in local currency (at the official exchange rate) for their imports or they receive from their central bank the local currency equivalent of their exports.

Price reform and realistic exchange rates imply that countries can afford to liberalize aggressively and to be quite free in the allocation of foreign exchange. It would be desirable, as a condition of membership, that countries maintain the same (dollar) exchange rate for trade in the union and with third countries.

Isn't there a risk that the system will not last very long? Structural deficit countries will quickly exhaust their reserves and that is the end of the mechanism.

Not so. When a country has used its full credit quota that simply means no further credit is available and all imbalances must be settled in hard currency. It still leaves for this country the benefit of multilateral offsetting and for everyone else that benefit plus the credit mechanism. In analogy with credit cards, people who have used up their credit line can still use their card, they just have to pay the bill at the end of the month.[2]

Does a payments mechanism free foreign exchange reserves?

Yes, since, for intrasystem use, there is no need to settle in hard currency (except in higher tranches). As a result, foreign exchange can be used rather than held. Precisely because foreign exchange needs are reduced and a temporal credit cushion is in place, countries do not need to follow overly defensive strategies as they would in a reserve shortage situation.

The reserve issue is particularly important for two reasons. First, when countries do not have access to external credit (and this is patently the case for the former USSR), reserve holdings are the only buffer. If reserve levels are low then trade and payments policies will be highly defensive and thus the uncoordinated system is forced into a low-trade mode. Second, intra-USSR trade is very high relative to external trade. Thus the gains from a regional payments mechanism are substantial.

Can countries pick their own exchange rate? What if they pick the wrong one?

Countries must learn to select an exchange rate at which their trade balances (except for transfers from the West). When they have deficits, spending must be reduced and competitiveness increased. There may be some room for temporary trade restrictions to achieve balance, but the discipline of the settlements mechanism will force countries to have exchange rates at which they can maintain external balance. Exchange rates have to be quite flexible so as to avoid having trade restrictions do most of the work.

How can the mechanism start to work if the new countries do not even have hard currency reserves?

The West, in funding the system, can put into the mechanism a starting pot. Participating countries will then discipline each other so that nobody overuses the endowment.

After so many years under the domination of Moscow, now that they are finally independent, should the new states not seek immediately a link with the West and get away from interrepublic trade? Is that not what Czechoslovakia and Poland did?

Trade with the West will certainly be an important feature of the emerging foreign trade pattern. But why sacrifice productive interrepublic trade? Instead, much of that trade can continue, once it is based on market prices rather than planners' mistakes. Eastern Europe will certainly make a serious mistake if it sacrifices opportunities in the East to narrow-minded nationalism. It is certainly better to have a prosperous neighbor than one whose collapse of trade leads to economic difficulties and political risk. The West will insist on economic cooperation as the quid pro quo for economic aid; it can accept limited trade discrimination (including in Eastern Europe) as a way of establishing a viable economic zone in the East.

The multilateral offsetting of balances and the credit mechanism are obviously attractive, but shouldn't the same trade policy be applied toward other republics and the rest of the world? Why favor members in the system?

In the case of the EPU, trade barriers were erected to protect scarce foreign exchange. Dollars were scarce since they represented access to capital goods and raw materials. In the Soviet Union, just as in Eastern Europe, there will be a shortage of foreign exchange unless real exchange rates are set at outright impoverishing levels. Some protection against the outside helps save at least part of the economic structure.

If the exchange rate is uniform and trade is open, what protects domestic economic activity?

The first answer is that a highly competitive exchange rate will. Imports will be very expensive and exports will be very profitable. Thus domestic production will be favored. But there is also a case for going further.

In a transition period, while agents learn to interact with the world economy, a protective tariff is appropriate. The case for a tariff lies in the experience of eastern Germany after reunification, where domestic goods were uniformly treated as "lemons"—everything from the West was better, even eggs. To avoid a wholesale collapse of demand for domestic goods, a competitive, uniform exchange rate can be supplemented with a uniform tariff that declines over a five-year period from 50 to 10 percent.

The argument for a tariff used here is a variant of that used to protect infant industries. It applies to the supply side, where learning to enhance product design and quality will make domestic products increasingly desirable over time. It also applies to the consumer, where the initial instinct to go all out for Western goods creates an externality since it involves a far more competitive exchange rate and lower real wage than would a "buy-USSR" effect induced by a tariff. But it is important to use a uniform tariff rather than quotas or licenses because the former USSR needs competition, even if it is only at the margin where a tariff ceases to offer protection.

A more depreciated exchange rate offers some of the opportunities afforded by a tariff, but not all. For one thing, a depreciation may soon be offset by wage inflation and thus not last. A tariff is a *real* intervention that protects a country against imports while implicitly taxing exports.

Could countries with convertible currencies participate in the mechanism? Specifically, could and should Poland or Slovakia be a member?

There is no reason for countries like Poland not to join and use the multilateral offsetting mechanism and the credit mechanism. Polish firms would take advantage only if it is profitable, and the same is true of the republics. The advantage is this: countries with inconvertible currencies that run deficits with Poland, if trade were settled in dollars, would be reluctant to let trade flourish even if they had surpluses in the system with other countries. Trade restrictions would needlessly kill off trade, whereas with a clearing mechanism the imbalances could be offset multilaterally. On the trade front, too, broadening the free trade area to include Eastern Europe would be in everybody's interest.

Is there any evidence from the experience of the EPU in the 1950s that a payments union slows down the progress toward convertibility?

Current account convertibility was achieved gradually in the 1950s. Countries with a persistently strong external balance, as for example Germany, moved ahead with trade liberalization. Other countries followed more gradually. Convertibility could have been achieved earlier, but that might have meant a less rapid and pervasive trade liberalization. The annual renewal of the EPU was at least a mechanism to keep an eye on the target of convertibility. Moreover, Switzerland was a member even though its currency was fully convertible. The EPU experience brings out the connection between trade and payments liberalization; trade restrictions may come off more rapidly if a payments arrangement makes countries less vulnerable to external balance swings.

Why does the IMF seem so ambivalent if not outright hostile toward such a system?

The same was true in the 1950s. The IMF adopted a hands-off policy with respect to the EPU, which was seen as a competing forum for policy discussion and surveillance. As a result, the IMF lost its effectiveness with respect to Western Europe. An extra factor might be this: the IMF is anxious to avoid the creation of new, bad monies, and this encourages a ruble zone and continuation of a Russia-centered system. The argument is reinforced if one takes the view that a ruble zone is a pragmatic counterpart to continued, substantial transfers from Russia to other republics. More likely, though, it is just avoiding serious questions. In any event, a few very bad monies (which is the current situation) might be even worse.

Conclusion

As central management weakens, there is a need to define national independence on the economic front. If the republics do not take the initiative in reforming, trade will inevitably collapse. And with the trade collapse may come a dramatic fall of all economic activity and public order. If they introduce new monies that turn out to be soft and thus inconvertible, trade problems will emerge almost immediately. Reserve shortages will soon lead to competitive trade restrictions.

Among the urgent priorities of a newly independent country is price liberalization to bring goods back to the market and into production. The price reform includes the choice of a realistic exchange rate. Another immediate step is the creation of a coordinating mechanism that bridges the borders and facilitates to the maximum the exchange of goods. Third in priority is monetary reform, including balancing the budget and dealing with the ruble overhang.

Most reforms have to do with the operation of the domestic economy—price liberalization, property rights, a domestic payments system, a stable money, etc.—where there is little role for outsiders. But the West *can* play an important role in the setting up of a payments union. The help of the West can come in three areas. First, in designing the technical setup and using utmost pressure (as the United States did in the creation of the EPU) to push the scheme ahead and get it implemented. This impetus is necessary because each internal party will seek modalities that meet its short-run situation and there is not much room to do this.

Second, the West can capitalize and guarantee the mechanism. This does not take much since most of the credit (except for special arrangements) is extended by the members. In the case of the EPU, the United States contributed capital of $270 million.[3]

Third, the West can administer the mechanism. This might be done by the BIS, as in the case of the EPU, or by a central bank such as the Bank of Sweden. But the agent would only keep the books. Just as in the case of the EPU, the burden of liberalizing and dealing with crises falls on the members who must learn how to live with one another.

Economic efficiency will thrive in a regime where convertibility comes soon. But if the margin for error in an immediate move to convertibility is very high, then it is much better that the change happen more gradually. Full convertibility in five years is better than a reaction against quick action that leads to trade restrictions and inconvertibility for a long time to come.

In addition, there are strong economic arguments in support of the proposition that the former USSR, and preferably all the countries of Eastern Europe, become a free trade zone. For quite a while they will be uncompetitive in world markets except at rock bottom real wages. In Russia today the monthly wage of workers is less than $20 per month. Even at that wage much of Russian industry is uncompetitive, and the same goes, of course, for the other republics. Is there a case for a preferential trading arrangement to move more gradually to free trade? The answer clearly is positive.

Member countries of the former COMECON should try to save some of the industries that may ultimately be viable by a regional trading arrangement. Some members of such a free trade area might want to maintain temporary restrictions on imports from the West. Of course, the economics is quite clear on the most efficient form of such restrictions, namely a uniform tariff at a moderate rate. Just to give a benchmark, some have argued 40 percent. This protection would help to offset the extraordinary advantages of the West along the lines of the infant industry argument.

The argument for a payments area thus has a parallel argument for a regional trade liberalization scheme, just as was the case in Western Europe.

5 The Progress of Restructuring in Poland

Restructuring in the economies of Eastern Europe must proceed simultaneously on three fronts. The first is the closing of those state firms—or more accurately those parts of state firms—that cannot adapt to the new conditions. The second is the transformation of those that can, but often only with an infusion of new capital. The third is the growth of new firms, of a brand new private sector. These fronts are not independent. Rapid growth of the private sector may partly substitute for the transformation of existing firms. Rapid growth of the private sector, and thus of private employment, also makes it easier to lay off workers and to close those state firms that need to be closed. Delays in closing state firms, on the other hand, through subsidies or other means, take resources away from the rest of the economy, slowing down the growth of the private sector. Put simply, successful restructuring requires that all three processes move forward at roughly consistent speeds, that neither gets sufficiently out of step to stop the adjustment process.

Written by Olivier Blanchard and Marek Dabrowski.

The role of governments in this restructuring process must be fundamentally threefold. They must first remove subsidies and allow prices to clear markets, so that prices can give the right signals as to what should and should not be produced. They must then credibly establish that, at those prices, the budget constraints faced by state firms have become truly hard, that the state will not come and bail out those that are failing. They must finally make sure that firms, now aware of the signals and the constraints, respond appropriately to these new incentives; to do so, they must put in place appropriate structures of ownership and control.

Looking at the major countries of Eastern Europe, Hungary, Czechoslovakia, and Poland, it is becoming clear that while governments have done surprisingly well with respect to the first two requirements, they have done poorly with respect to the third. Price liberalization and the reduction of subsidies were technically simple measures, which could be done nearly at the stroke of a pen. What they required were steady nerves and enough political consensus. Those were there, and those economies now operate under market-clearing prices and considerably reduced subsidies. Establishing the credibility of the hard budget constraint could have proven harder to achieve. After all, the reform programs of the early 1990s had been preceded by many earlier attempts, which had not changed the status quo very much. But things were perceived this time to be fundamentally different, and credibility of the budget constraint was largely and quickly established.[1] The third role has proven much harder to fill. In contrast to, say, price liberalization, privatization of state firms was an inherently complex task, in mostly uncharted territory. And, in most countries, only a small minority of the large state firms have moved from state to private hands. The others exist in limbo, unwilling and unable to take the decisions that would be needed to restructure and survive.

As a result, the transformation of state firms has happened very slowly. Most state firms, including those that should be saved, in part or in total, are still declining. Some are on the verge of collapse. The new private sector, as well as it is doing, cannot grow fast or wide enough to take up the slack. Unemployment is growing, and so is the duration of unemployment; there are few jobs for those who lose their jobs in state firms. Pressure to prop up state firms, to slow down their decline, is mounting. And some of the countries, in particular Poland which started earlier than the others, are at a crucial crossroad.

Faced with the social and political implications of letting large state firms close, often in regions that are already doing poorly, governments may try to avoid or at least delay the outcome through subsidies, ad hoc tariffs, and other measures. The experience of Western countries and their inability to close declining industries, from shipyards to mines, comes to mind here. But, if this road is taken, the drain on resources will threaten macrostabilization. And even if a short-run crisis is avoided, the diversion of resources for such uses is likely to slow down the growth of the private sector, and eventually to derail restructuring.

Or the governments can stand firm, keep the budget constraint hard, and let state firms decline and close. This is clearly the only road that eventually leads to growth. But, for this to happen, those jobs that should be saved must be saved, those firms that need capital for restructuring must get it, and those workers who lose jobs must get minimum protection. Otherwise, the outcome is likely to be much higher unemployment and a strong backlash against the reform process.

The focus of this chapter will be on restructuring, its evolution, and the choices to be made. Rather than giving a general description, the focus will be on Poland, with occasional references to other Eastern European countries. This makes for an easier narrative, and while the details vary, the general issues are common to those countries that have achieved the first phase of reform, stabilization and liberalization. In a number of respects, the case of Poland is the most informative. Poland started earlier, so there are nearly three years of transition to learn from. Stabilization and price liberalization were carried out fully a year before the full collapse of CMEA trade, allowing for an easier characterization of the effects of each one. And one of the more positive legacies of central planning, which has endured to this day, is the collection of detailed information on firms, making it easier to form an accurate picture of their evolution.

The chapter first examines the initial response of firms to reform, and documents the effects of price liberalization and the establishment of the hard budget constraint. We then describe the slow progress on privatization and analyze its causes. The third section examines the behavior of state firms, and how the lack of progress on privatization has led to both their unwillingness and their inability to take the steps needed to restructure. The next documents the fast growth but also the limits and problems of the emerging private sector. The last two sections focus on the choices at hand. We first document the steady softening of the budget constraint throughout 1991, and how, at the end of 1991, it looked increasingly likely that Poland would choose the first road, that the reform process might be derailed. Despite a series of weak governments, those worries have proven unfounded, and now, with the appointment of a stronger government, restructuring looks poised to move forward. Finally we discuss the measures to be taken. In particular, we present and assess current plans on privatization, the cleanup of the banking system, and the social treatment of unemployment.

The Initial Reform Program and the Behavior of Firms

As Poland embarked in January 1990 on price liberalization and macrostabilization, there were widespread fears that state firms, which had never operated in a market economy, would respond in perverse fashion. They would, the argument went, keep on producing even in the face of declining sales, pay workers wages in excess of revenues, borrow from state banks and assume that the state would, as before, come to the rescue. The state would indeed eventually have no choice than to do just that and bail them out, validating their initial expectations. The end result would be a macroeconomic crisis and the failure of macrostabilization.

Those fears turned out to be unjustified (though the same fears are unfortunately proving justified in Russia). Stabilization and liberalization were quickly followed by a sharp drop in output, but it had little to do with perverse responses of state firms. While our focus is not on the initial contraction in output, this nevertheless is a central feature of the adjustment, and we briefly review it before turning to the behavior of state firms in the initial phase of reform.[2]

The Output Decline

Stabilization and price liberalization were implemented on 1 January 1990.[3] Rationing was gone nearly overnight. But there was also a quick and sharp decline in output. The decline in sales by the "socialized sector" was equal to 20 percent in January, to 23 percent for the first quarter of 1991. Its broad causes are now well understood. The decline in output was mainly the result of an adverse shift in aggregate demand, and to a lesser extent of a shift in relative demand.

Stabilization was associated with a large increase in prices, an increase that was larger than forecast but in retrospect can be explained as the result of cost-plus pricing in the face of the reduction of subsidies, the increase in administered prices, and high nominal interest rates on working capital.

Higher prices and tight money resulted in a reduction in real money and real credit and helped cause a decrease in aggregate demand. The second cause of this was a much larger than expected fiscal surplus, due to high profit taxes. Again, in retrospect, this is easily explained. Pricing of inputs at historical cost, combined with a large increase in prices, led to large paper profits by firms, leading in turn to large profit tax payments. The effect was a large transfer of income from firms and workers to the state, and a decrease in aggregate demand. Larger than expected increases in prices, unexpected fiscal revenues, and a large output decline were also the outcome in Czechoslovakia and Bulgaria when they implemented their stabilization plan a year later (Bruno 1992).

How much this shift in aggregate demand was compounded by a shift in relative demand, away from goods produced by state firms and toward privately produced goods or imports, is an important question; put another way, it is the question of whether the initial decline in output was an unfortunate implication of stabilization, or was instead part and parcel of the restructuring process—as it was for example in East Germany, where demand shifted overnight away from domestic goods. There were good reasons to expect that stabilization and liberalization would be associated with shifts in relative demand, away from those products that had been sold only because of large subsidies, or because of forced substitution (Winiecki 1990). But, overall, the evidence does not support the view that this was the dominant part of the decrease in demand.

Within the state sector, some sectors were affected more than others; but sales in nearly all sectors were down. Somewhat surprisingly given that Poland, like other Eastern European economies, had too high a share of production in heavy manufacturing, the decline in sales was larger in light than in heavy industry. This is because, in 1990, heavy industry continued to benefit from both cheap CMEA imports of energy and raw materials and continuing export possibilities to other CMEA countries, and thus was less affected by the domestic demand contraction; in 1991, with the collapse of CMEA and the adjustment of energy prices, the situation of heavy industry deteriorated substantially. As to the shift between goods produced by state and by private firms, the evidence is that those private firms that existed at the start of stabilization also fared poorly, although not quite as poorly as state firms. But those private firms often were either exploiting arbitrage opportunities present in the previous regime and eliminated by reform, or were nearly parasitic, highly dependent on state firms themselves. As to the new private sector, the explosion of street vendors in Warsaw became the stuff of newspaper headlines at the time. As to the shift toward foreign goods, the published numbers on imports do not show an import boom; but there is again considerable evidence that many imports, including some that made their way in the trunks of cars from Germany, were not recorded. Even with generous allowances for undermeasurement however, the reading of the evidence must be that the decline in output was mostly the result of a shift in aggregate demand rather than in relative demand.

The Reaction of State Firms

Our interest here is in how the state firms reacted both to the reform measures and to the drop in demand. Part of the reform program was a clear signal by the government of a change in the rules of the game governing relations between state firms and the state. Subsidies were slashed; firms were told that they could no longer expect ad hoc transfers from the budget. Assets serving as the base for the "dividend tax" were revalued, with failure to pay the tax made a potential trigger for starting liquidation proceedings. The old bankruptcy laws of 1934 were dusted off. The evidence is that, by and large, the signals were widely judged credible, and that firms acted under the assumption that the budget constraints had indeed suddenly become hard. Two examples are particularly striking.

The first is the setting of nominal wages by firms at the start of stabilization. Part of the reform package was an incomes policy, put in place to avoid excessive wage payments by firms to their workers. While wage payments under the policy were not particularly generous, allowing only for limited indexation to the initial price increases, wages were, for the first few months after the start of reform, set far below the guidelines. There are two explanations as to why this was. The first is uncertainty, the desire of firms, in the face of an unknown transition process, to play it safe and thus to generate more than sufficient profits to avoid bankruptcy. The other is that, despite the fact that firms had high accounting profits early on in stabilization, they also had low cash flows, forcing them to keep wages low. The explanation for this seemingly contradictory behavior of profits and cash flows is the same as for the budget surplus mentioned earlier. Accounting profits were high because of accounting of inputs by firms at historical—and thus much lower nominal—costs; the large taxes that firms thus had to pay as a result of high accounting profits were enough to nearly wipe out cash flows. Whatever the reason, whether uncertainty or low cash flows, the hard budget constraint, current or prospective, was thus a source of wage moderation.

The second example is the adjustment of production to sales. The initial decrease in sales was associated with an initial buildup of inventories. But within less than a month, firms had cut production below sales, and both trade and industry were decumulating inventories. Again there was a quick adjustment of firms to the realities of the market, the need for smaller inventory levels in an economy with market-clearing prices, and to the fact of hard budget constraints.

Both of these features have also characterized the other Eastern European stabilization episodes. But, interestingly, the glimpses we have of the reaction of Russian firms to the start of the reform process there suggest a different response, with firms keeping production at the planned level and accumulating inventories in the presence of declining sales. While this may come from 70 rather than 40 years of central planning, an alternative and more likely explanation is that the credibility of the program and thus of the hard budget constraint is much lower in Russia than it was in Eastern Europe at the beginning of stabilization.

Operating under a budget constraint is not, however, the same as profit maximizing. In the absence of any clear owner, workers and managers were left de facto in charge of firms, an issue to which we return at length later. And, while production was quickly scaled down, employment was not, reflecting the strong weight of workers in the decisions of state firms. Three months into reform, labor productivity was sharply down from the already low pre-reform level. With the lack of progress on privatization, the role of workers was, if anything, going to become stronger, shaping the decisions of the firms in the following two years. In the next two sections, we discuss first the stalling of privatization and then the behavior of state firms over the two years following reform.

The Slow Progress on Privatization

While thinking about privatization had started as early as the mid-1980s in Poland, the passage of a specific privatization program was left to after the start of reform. Once municipal ownership was reestablished and new local governments were in place in the spring of 1990, privatization of shops proceeded steadily. By the end of 1991, privatization of shops was largely accomplished. But the progress has been much slower for the privatization of firms, in particular large state firms. At the start of stabilization, there were about 8,500 such firms, with 1,000 employing more than 1,000 employees. At the end of 1991, only about 10 percent of them had been privatized.

The Methods of Privatization

After 24 drafts and an intense debate in Parliament, a privatization law was passed in July 1990.[4] It provided for privatization both from the top down, that is at the initiative of the Ministry of Privatization, and from the bottom up, at the initiative of firms, alone or in combination with creditors and potential buyers.

The general philosophy in top-down privatization was to sell firms to the highest bidder. The initial effort in top-down privatization was to prepare companies for initial public offerings, or IPOs. After a process of winnowing, five companies, accounting for 23,000 employees, were offered to the public in November 1990. Despite initial hopes that the rate of sales would increase, only an additional five IPOs were conducted in 1991. In 1991, the strategy was changed to put more emphasis on sectoral privatization, with the idea of using economies of scale in valuation, information, and organization of sales. The emphasis was also changed from IPOs to direct sales to buyers, considering not only price but business plans, employment guarantees, repayment of debt, and so on. By August 1992, however, a grand total of only 40 firms had been sold through these routes (including 14 by IPOs). The total value of firms sold in this way, known as "capital privatization," was $250 million, about 0.3 percent of GDP. New top down privatization plans, in particular a plan known slightly misleadingly given its current limited scope as "mass privatization," have been developed and are ready to go. They have not started yet, and we shall discuss them later.

The 1990 law also provided for bottom-up privatization, through a channel known as "liquidation." Under that approach, workers and managers, and outside investors as the case may be, submit a plan for the sale of the firm to the Ministry of Privatization. If the plan is approved, they pay 10 percent of the estimated value of the firm—often the book value, with minor adjustments—and lease the rest from the state for a period of 15 years, at a rate substantially below market. Liquidation in effect represents a discounted sale to insiders. Because one of the requirements is that the initial capital of the new firm be equal to 20 percent of the estimated value of the firm, this route has been followed only in small and medium-size firms; by August 1992, liquidation according to the 1990 law had been followed by about 500 firms, only 20 percent of which employed more than 500 workers. It has been used mostly for management or worker and management buyouts, as the ministry proved reluctant to offer such attractive terms to outsiders, especially to foreign investors.

Two other channels were already available to firms before the privatization law of 1990, and both have been used as well.

The first is to sell individual assets. To prevent the prere-form nomenklatura privatizations in which managers could in effect appropriate their firms, a law was passed in 1989 that made liquidation mandatory if more than half of the assets of the firms were in some way transferred or sold to another firm. Thus, managers could in principle sell up to half of their assets without authorization. While this allowed for a flexible way for firms to dispose of unneeded assets, fear of income distribution implications and political considerations led in 1991 to a tightening of requirements, in effect requiring managers to obtain permission from their "founding organ" before disposing of firms' assets. There is some evidence that state firms have indeed sold or leased part of their capital, a phenomenon sometimes referred to as invisible privatization. In a recent survey of 75 large state firms, 22 of them reported selling or leasing productive assets, but the share of assets involved was small, between 1 and 5 percent, never exceeding 10 percent (Pinto, Bella, and Krajewski 1992). In another survey, this time of private firms (Webster 1992), all private manufacturing firms had bought their (secondhand) machines from state firms.

The second channel is to start liquidation according to the state enterprise law of 1981. While this was intended as a bankruptcy procedure for firms, initiated by the firms themselves, it has in practice sometimes resembled the first type of liquidation, leading to the creation of a new firm, with write-down of old debts. By August 1992, this route had been followed by about 750 firms, again most of them small and medium-size; only 10 percent had more than 500 employees.

Why Privatization Has Been So Slow

The first delay in privatization was due simply to the long time it took to put a general framework in place. Nearly a year went by before the mechanics of privatization were settled. Five months, from late 1989 to March 1990, were spent in internal discussions within the Ministry of Finance and within the government. The debate then moved to Parliament for another five months. The reasons were twofold: the very complexity of the proposed schemes, and their distributional implications. In particular, in a country where unions had played an essential role in the transition, the question of how much control should be given to workers, on both distribution and efficiency grounds, was the subject of bitter debates (Dabrowski 1991b). Many of the power plays currently taking place in Russia, discussed in chapter 3 of this report, were instead carried out in discussions within the government and later in Parliament.

The passage of a privatization law was an important step. But, while it set up general principles, it could not settle once and for all disagreements and relative claims. Many of the delays since mid-1990 clearly reflect those latent tensions. There have been five changes at the head of the Ministry of Privatization,[5] with each minister having his own ideas as to the best privatization strategy. Changes in ministers and chronic underfunding have led to organizational confusion within the ministry. Other ministries, in particular the Ministry of Trade and Industry, have fought hard to retain whatever control they could on state firms, leading to numerous conflicts of competence between them and the Ministry of Privatization. But the main problems in implementing privatization have been mostly of a different, more logistical nature. Those in turn are traceable to two characteristics of state firms. First, state firms are difficult to value; accounting is poor and many claims are legally ill defined, or their value hard to assess. Second, large state firms, in contrast to their Western counterparts, are collections of activities, many of them—housing, transportation, repair services—only tangential to their central activity, at least in the new market environment. And of their main activities, typically only a few can and should survive, and the others must close. These two characteristics have affected both top-down and bottom-up privatization, in different ways:

In top-down privatization, the main difficulty has been the problem of valuation. The cost of valuing firms for the first five IPOs was an extremely high 20 percent of their value. There is a clear tradeoff between care in valuation and speed of privatization. Simple valuation procedures are de facto more likely to benefit buyers—and often insiders—and thus to lead to fast privatization. Careful valuation avoids abuses, but slows down the process.[6] In the case of capital privatization in Poland, all the incentives lead to careful valuation and very slow speed. Civil servants have little or nothing to gain from speed, but a lot to lose from agreeing to deals that turn out to have been too beneficial to the buyers. They can actually be held criminally responsible for such a deal, and, after the fall of the Bielecki government, a number of sales were indeed examined for signs of potential excess generosity. Overly careful valuation and prudent decisions have been the primary reasons why top-down privatization has been so slow.

The heterogeneity of activities within firms has also played a role, however. Buyers who were usually interested in one or two of the main activities of a particular firm have been reluctant to take on the whole firm. There is an important lesson here about restructuring and privatization. That debate has often been cast in terms of a choice between whether a firm should be restructured and then privatized, or instead privatized and then restructured. Stated as such, this is a misleading debate. Restructuring of a firm in the context of privatization may mean two different things. The first is the rough cutting up of the various activities, so that each is relatively homogeneous and can be sold—or closed—separately. The second is the in-depth reorganization and transformation of some of these activities so that they can compete in domestic and foreign markets. There is no question that the second should happen after privatization: the state surely has no comparative advantage over the buyer in doing so. Looking at how the firms sold through IPOs have done since is quite revealing in this respect. While they were chosen on the basis of their apparently bright prospects, many of them have done poorly. This is not, it appears, because of poor management but rather because the assessment of their prospects was not particularly accurate.[7] But, as to the first stage of restructuring, the evidence from the Polish experience and elsewhere is that simple cutting up considerably facilitates privatization.[8]

Heterogeneity of activities rather than valuation has been the main obstacle in bottom-up privatization. In the very large firms, the coordination needed to achieve a coalition between managers and workers has proven simply too difficult to achieve. More importantly, consensus has proven difficult to achieve in those cases—in effect, the large majority—where it was clear that only some parts of the firm could be saved, and the others phased out. While it is easy to think of schemes that would have winners compensate losers, for example by giving laid-off workers either a cash payment or a title to some of the profits of the new firm, those schemes have not arisen. Thus, in many cases, the consensus required to start and achieve liquidation has not been achieved. (And, as we already mentioned, in some cases where consensus was achieved at the bottom, the process was stopped at the top, because of the reluctance of civil servants to approve deals that favored insiders.) The difficulty of achieving a coalition in the face of divergent interests appears to have been so far the main bottleneck in Polish bottom-up privatization.

To sum up the analysis so far, price liberalization has created the incentives for new activities. Price liberalization together with the hard budget constraint have forced state firms to adjust to those new realities. But, with the slow progress on privatization, the transformation of state firms, the third leg of the general restructuring process, has lagged behind. The next two sections deal first with the evolution of state firms and then with the growth of the private sector.

The Evolution of State Firms

The Emergence of Workers' Control

The experiences of Poland and other Eastern European countries make clear that the absence of privatization is not synonymous with maintained control of the state.[9] In some countries, managers have found themselves de facto in charge; in others, workers have found themselves in that role. In Poland, a latent structure of workers' control had been put in place in the reform of 1981. As long, however, as managers had the backing of the center, those councils did not play a dominant role.[10] But with the fall of the Communist government in the summer of 1989, the councils took on progressively more power, including the ability to hire and fire managers. This tendency was reinforced over the following two years. Elections for new councils in 1990 were often followed by referenda on the management. By the end of 1990, half of all managing directors had been confirmed by elections, 40 percent of these new.[11]

Workers' control of a firm is not necessarily bad. Indeed, firms with workers as shareholders have incentives that are roughly aligned with those of firms with outside owners.[12] But two elements, both linked to the lack of progress on privatization, have played a much more important and detrimental role than workers' control per se. First, workers have control but not ownership; the uncertainty about their eventual stake in the firm after privatization has made them reluctant to invest in the future. The privatization law of 1990 promised them only 20 percent at half price, not enough to justify large sacrifices for a small and uncertain reward. Second, and again because of the uncertainty about ultimate ownership, firms have found it difficult in their current status to attract the capital and the expertise needed to turn them around. Indeed, they have often lost their best and most motivated workers and managers to the private sector. Thus, for both reasons, state firms have acted with short horizons, taking the measures needed to avoid immediate closure but not those needed to survive and to grow.[13]

The Behavior of State Firms

First, state firms have tried to preserve jobs, limiting whenever they could the rate of employment decline to the rate of attrition. In 1990, while separations increased slightly, hirings collapsed. Thus, unemployment has disproportionately affected new entrants in the labor force. In 1991, 45 percent of new graduates went from school to the unemployment rolls; 32 percent of the unemployed were 18–24 years old. And only 20 percent of the unemployed were unemployed because of group layoffs.[14] As time passes, however, and some firms are forced to take more drastic measures, group layoffs are playing a more important role. Part of the reduction in employment has also been achieved through early retirement. The increase in pensioners in 1991 was 1.1 million, whereas the size of the cohort of workers reaching normal retirement age was only 200,000. Given the sharp declines in output, both at the time of stabilization and then one year later in response to the breakdown of the CMEA, labor productivity in industry, which was already low at the beginning of reform, was nearly 20 percent lower at the end of 1991. By the beginning of 1992, however, it was starting to improve.

Second, firms have steadily transferred revenues to wages. After their initial prudence in setting wages, firms quickly raised them to the level allowed by the incomes policy, and then even further, by being increasingly willing to pay the excess wage tax, or *popiwek;* as a result, the tax has been an unexpectedly large source of state revenues, accounting for 14 percent of state tax revenues in 1991. The main factor limiting the speed at which this transfer has taken place has been incomes policy, which has however only slowed the transfer.[15] Thus, measured profit rates have steadily decreased. From 31 percent at the beginning of 1990, markups (the ratio of sales minus costs to costs) went down to 24 percent at the end of 1990, and to 13 percent at the end of 1991.[16] In the first quarter of 1992, 35 percent of the firms had negative gross profits. And from the middle of 1991 a new ominous trend appeared, that of firms accumulating both interest and tax arrears, thus testing the hard budget constraint. This is an important development, and one we return at more length later.

Paralysis, or Weeding Out?

That the state sector is doing badly at this point is not per se a sign of failure of the reform process. Indeed, if privatization had proceeded on schedule, and if restructuring was proceeding at a steady pace, the aggregate picture of the state sector might not look very different. Many state firms would have closed, or be on the verge of closing, and many others would be shedding unprofitable activities. The general picture would also be one of low average profits, quite possibly of lower output—though probably of higher rather than lower labor productivity. But the aggregate picture would hide a reality of heterogeneous fortunes, with some firms, perhaps a minority, adapting and starting to grow.[17] Such does not appear to be the case. There were signs in early 1990 that most firms were considering partnerships with foreign firms, development of marketing activities, and various degrees of restructuring.[18] But as the employment implications of restructuring as well as the difficulties of entering joint ventures, finding outside capital, and so on became clearer, most firms gave up such efforts. There are a few examples of state firms that are adapting, sometimes with managers obtaining compensation schemes with strong incentives. But these examples remain isolated. Review of the evidence at the sectoral level does not show much heterogeneity across sectors. Sales are down in nearly all sectors. The dispersion of profit rates across 3-digit sectors in industry has fallen steadily since the end of 1989. Indeed, a puzzling feature of the adjustment is that there is simply no correlation between the actual performance of sectors and the predictions that had been made earlier on the basis of computations such as value added at world prices per unit of output. This may, however, reflect more on the reliability of such computations than on the nature of the adjustment.[19] One relatively bright note is the behavior of exports. The rate of growth of exports (state and private, but private exports probably did not account for much in 1990) to the EEC in dollars was a striking 65 percent in 1990; it was very much across the board, suggesting a low exchange rate, rather than new products and new markets, as the primary cause of the boom. The rate of growth was still a respectable 13 percent in 1991, but most state firms, which were not involved in finding foreign customers under the previous regime, still appear to be poor at doing so.

The Growth of the Private Sector

The overall growth of the private sector has been spectacular, even more so in Poland that in other Eastern European countries. In December 1988, recorded private employment outside of agriculture was equal to 1.2 million. With the passage of a law removing most restrictions on entry in December 1988—thus a full year before the start of reform—private employment had already increased at the start of stabilization to 1.8 million. By the end of 1991 it stood at 3.0 million, or roughly 26 percent of total nonagricultural employment.[20] Including agriculture, which was mostly private already, close to half of the population is now working in the private sector.[21]

The Growth in Trade, Services, and Constructions

Not surprisingly, this growth has been stronger in those sectors that had traditionally been repressed. In trade the private sector accounted for 75 percent of sales at the end of 1991, compared to 10 percent at the end of 1989. Much of this increase reflects the privatization of trade that took place during the period. But some of it reflects the creation of new firms: total employment growth in trade, private and state, was equal to 16 percent in 1991. The private sector has also become dominant in construction. At the end of 1991, private sector sales accounted for half of total sales, up from a quarter in 1989. By contrast, in industry, the private sector accounted for only 18 percent of sales, up from 7 percent in 1989.

Also not surprisingly, much of the growth has been in very small businesses. Official statistics distinguish between three types of private businesses, joint ventures (firms with some foreign capital), domestic firms, and individual businesses. The rate of growth of all three over 1990–1991 was roughly the same. But because individual businesses represented more than 80 percent of employment at the start, this implies that more than 80 percent of the growth of employment over 1990–1991 was in individual businesses. Average employment in those was only 1.7 workers.

That the Polish economy needed more trade, services, and construction is not at issue. But, given how little restructuring has happened in state firms in manufacturing, the question arises of whether and to what extent growth of the private sector can substitute for the restructuring of state firms. Kornai has long argued that only the new private sector not the existing state sector, can be counted on to be the engine of growth in Eastern Europe. But, based on the existing evidence, private firms in manufacturing clearly cannot be expected, any time soon, to substitute for the transformation of existing state firms. Modern manufacturing is too large and too sophisticated to be developed quickly from scratch, especially with limited foreign participation.

The Growth in Manufacturing

Private manufacturing is still small. The converse side of the statistics given earlier is that employment in larger private domestic firms, with or without foreign capital, while increasing at high rates, only accounted for 500,000 workers in mid-1991, up from 250,000 before stabilization. The evidence from aggregate data and from surveys gives a fairly clear view of those firms.

Behind the term "private sector" lies a hodgepodge of firms with very different characteristics. An important distinction is between firms created before and after reform. Many of the firms set up before the reform were created to exploit some flaw in the previous system—pricing leading to quasi-arbitrage opportunities, shortages—or to allow activities normally under the purview of state firms to be conducted for private profit instead. The private sector companies that existed before stabilization (about 1,500 industrial companies, with an employment of about 29,000 people in 1989) did better than state firms during stabilization, but not much better; their real sales in particular were down by 2 percent in 1990. Many of those firms were made obsolete by price liberalization, and have either closed or moved on to other activities. The firms created since the reform have typically been created by what Webster refers to as "technicians"—in contrast to "opportunists" earlier—engineers and managers of state firms who concluded that they could produce either a better product or at a lower cost than the firms they had worked in previously. Those are the firms from which growth is likely to come.

Private firms do not exist in a domestic vacuum, importing inputs from abroad and selling their production as exports. Most of the firms examined in the World Bank survey (Webster 1992) were either buying more than 50 percent of their inputs from or supplying more than 50 percent of their output to state firms. Thus, the demise of state firms can clearly lead to the demise of many of these private firms. One cannot make the assumption that the private sector will grow in a vacuum: restructuring of state firms is clearly essential to the growth of the private sector.

Most of the firms analyzed in the World Bank survey were suffering from a number of problems that limited their growth. All were internally financed initially, although the majority were using short-term credit as well. Interestingly, in view of the behavior of banks we shall take up below, few reported problems in obtaining bank loans. (Indeed, some of the loans made by state-owned banks to private firms were made without adequate collateral, leading to some spectacular failures later on.) Many, however, found the cost of credit much too high. Indeed, for those who were exporting to the West and did not have access to foreign credit, pegging of the nominal exchange rate from January 1990 to May 1991 implied that zloty nominal interest rates were the relevant measure of the cost of credit; and nominal interest rates during that period were indeed very high. All these firms were using capital equipment they had bought from either ongoing or bankrupt state firms; this equipment was in most cases old, making it harder for them to be competitive on world markets. And this general impression of a set of firms struggling to be competitive with little expertise and relatively old equipment is consistent with the numbers on foreign direct investment. Foreign direct investment in Poland has increased steadily since reform. But in 1991, estimated flows for all foreign investment were still well below 0.5 percent of GDP. The growth of the private sector in Poland is still largely a domestic affair.

The Reemergence of the Soft Budget Constraint

Faced with the threat of widespread closing of plants and firms, governments are likely to be under strong pressure to slow down reform, to subsidize and to protect jobs in state firms. Throughout 1991, there were signs that firms were increasingly testing their budget constraint, and finding that they could indeed get away with it. Interest arrears were accumulating at commercial banks; tax arrears were steadily increasing, adding to an already serious fiscal crisis. In effect, many firms were paying wages but little else. At the end of 1991 in Poland it looked increasingly as if the government was starting to yield to pressure.

Mounting Arrears

The very high inflation at the end of 1989 had mostly eliminated debt liabilities of firms to banks, in effect wiping the
slates clean. But by the end of 1991, about 30 percent of the
loans made by commercial banks were again nonperforming. Interest payments were increasingly capitalized; interest arrears were up by 35 percent (in nominal terms) over
the last six months of 1991.

That firms were trying not to pay interest is easy to understand. There were two reasons, the first that those firms that
knew they had no future were playing an end game, no
longer valuing their relation to banks and their status as
borrowers, the second that firms expected the government
eventually to bail them out and declare some form of debt
consolidation. The more interesting question is why banks
were willing to extend further credit, or at least to capitalize
interest. Commercial banks in Poland, as elsewhere in Eastern Europe, are a recent and somewhat artificial creation.
The standard monobank of a Soviet-type economy was broken up in January 1989 into a central bank and 9 commercial
banks. Those banks have remained state-owned, and have
only recently been commercialized. Thus, a natural question
is whether their behavior can be attributed to state ownership or to other factors.

The answer is that both played a role. Those banks with
long dealings with state firms had a natural inclination,
whether or not it was wise, to keep lending to them. And
state banks are also surely more amenable to political pres-

sure. In June 1992, for example, there was explicit pressure by the then prime minister to make a loan to a firm to pay higher wages and avoid a politically damaging strike.[22] But the behavior of banks in Western economies suggests that more was at work. Banks everywhere are reluctant to admit to losses, and are likely to throw good money after bad, to capitalize arrears to make their balance sheet look better for a while. The argument has been made that even profit-maximizing banks may have an incentive to further lend to firms on new projects, as by doing so they may be able to recoup some of their losses on previous loans;[23] the argument is probably of limited quantitative relevance in the case of Poland, as there is little evidence that new loans were made beyond capitalization, or that borrowing firms were involved in new investment projects. Finally, it is likely that banks, just like firms, were expecting an eventual bailout, and thus were only moderately concerned about nonperforming loans.

Banks are not the only ones against which arrears were accumulated. Firms also accumulated tax arrears. Part of the initial reform plan was the revaluation of firms' assets, and making nonpayment of the tax on those assets, the "divi-denda," a trigger for liquidation proceedings. For most of the first year of reform, taxes were paid on time, and tax arrears were not an important issue. Throughout 1991, however, it became clear that some firms were testing the commitment of the government. By the end of 1991, tax arrears accounted for 12 percent of total tax revenues for 1991. For some taxes, the ratio was substantially higher. For the *popiwek* in particular, arrears amounted to nearly half of tax payments:[24] thus some firms were not only paying their workers more than the wage norm, but also not paying the penalties that they incurred by doing so. The explanation for why firms were following such behavior is the same as earlier, a combination of end game behavior and of the belief that the government would eventually forgive arrears.

More generally, one striking aspect of the transformation in Poland, in light of the growth of involuntary interenterprise credit, interest and tax arrears, has been the relatively small number of bankruptcies. We have suggested reasons why some creditors were reluctant to start bankruptcy proceedings. There is another, more mundane but very relevant explanation: bankruptcy is not a simple process in Poland.[25] The bankruptcy law dates from 1934. There is an extreme shortage of those judges and trustees who are required to carry out the bankruptcy proceedings. Thus, given the complexity of legal claims, bankruptcy proceedings necessarily take a long time. In addition, in response to the request by a creditor to start bankruptcy proceedings, the firm can petition the judge for an "arrangement," a counterproposal for reorganization of a firm. In effect, given the burden that this puts on the courts, the need to appoint judges, trustees, and supervisors as well as to study claims, proposals, and counterproposals, "arrangements" have been used by debtor firms to delay, often endlessly, the bankruptcy process. In anticipation of such delays, creditors are reluctant to start the process at all. This problem, in effect the difficulties in enforcing the hard budget constraint, has no simple solution. A new, streamlined bankruptcy law is in preparation.[26] But the lack of competent personnel will be there for a long time.

The Temptation Resisted

Given the mounting arrears, the departure of Leszek Balcerowitz from the Ministry of Finance in late 1991, and the weakness of the governments that followed, there were good reasons to fear that the budget constraint would soften further. When it comes to not paying taxes there is safety in numbers, and once firms found they could avoid paying taxes with impunity, it appeared likely that many would join in. From nonpayment of taxes to explicit subsidies is a small step, and the state could soon find itself supporting state firms on a large scale. This promised to add to an already large fiscal deficit, and eventually to more money creation.

These fears turn out, at least for this time, to have been unfounded. While the first half of 1992 was indeed a time of political turmoil, the credibility of the hard budget constraint has been reestablished. Tax arrears have decreased in real terms, and so have interest arrears. The government has gone after some tax avoiders, and banks have become reluctant to extend credit to those firms with arrears. There are signs that state firms have now taken as likely that the state will not come to the rescue. Group layoffs are increasing. Wages are below the norm allowed by the incomes policy in those firms that are making losses. How was the government able to achieve such a feat? One tentative explanation is that the dismal fiscal situation has, at least for these purposes, been a blessing in disguise. Because of the disappearance of profits in 1991, profit taxes have gone from 14 percent of GDP to 6 percent in 1991; with them state and local revenues have gone from 32.5 percent in 1990 to 26.3 percent in 1991. Under those conditions, it has become quite clear that the state can ill afford to pay subsidies.

Thus, for the time being, Poland is still on the path of reform and restructuring. But this path is not an easy one. And, as we have argued, in the absence of progress on the transformation of state firms, the likelihood of success appears small. The state sector will collapse and the private sector cannot be expected to pick up the slack. In the last section, we discuss the measures that must soon be taken.

The Measures to Be Taken

Accelerating Privatization

Acceleration of privatization is essential to the transformation of state firms. There are a number of new plans in store for privatization in Poland. The question is whether they will be more successful than those that have been in place since 1990.

The first, which was elaborated in 1991, was approved by the new government in August 1992 and is now in Parliament where it is not expected to be approved before February 1993. It is known as "mass privatization." It creates intermediaries that hold shares of firms, and are themselves held by the public.[27] While some details still have to be settled, the broad outline is as follows. The program will include about 400 companies, each with an average of about 1,000 employees. It will thus cover under 6 percent of state sector employment. The companies in the program will first be corporatized, transformed into joint stock companies, and their shares allocated 10 percent to the workers, 30 percent temporarily to the Treasury, and 60 percent to the newly created investment funds. The investment funds will total 10 to 20, and will be set up under the supervision of the Ministry of Privatization. They will be run by largely foreign staffs, with an experience in restructuring firms. Each fund will be the leading shareholder in about 20 companies, holding 33 percent of the shares, and a minority shareholder in the others. Shares in the investment funds will be distributed to the people, and will be tradable after some period of time; at this stage, the expected date is 1994.

The second plan is sectoral privatization, the pace of which is expected to accelerate. Studies of many sectors have now been completed and contracts taken with potential foreign buyers. The approach will favor direct sales over auctions, and will consider other factors than sales price, such as investment plans and employment guarantees.

The third, which is at an earlier stage of development, is known as privatization through restructuring. As currently defined, it will invite bids from management companies for the right to restructure a state firm. The firm will be allocated to the highest bidder, which will then have a given number of years to restructure and sell the state firm. The compensation of the company will be proportional to the difference between the proceeds from sales and the initial bid.

These approaches will coexist with liquidation, which will remain an option for firms that want to privatize. Because the current approach leads to a highly leveraged privatized firm, a firm with relatively large lease payments to the state, it leads to a high risk of bankruptcy and has made it difficult for those firms to borrow further in order to, for example, buy new capital equipment. Thus proposals are being considered to change the lease terms, either by changing them to an equity position of the state or by changing the time pattern of payments.

One clear lesson from the past two years is that one should endorse rather than criticize this abundance of methods. While we and many others have offered neat, all-encompassing schemes, the reality has been that they require too much consensus, too much expertise, and have not happened anywhere. Even in what was Czechoslovakia, voucher privatization is only one of a number of approaches, and has only been applied at this point to about 10 percent of state firms. A range of methods, despite its seeming anarchy, holds the best promise of achieving privatization.

This does not imply that all approaches are acceptable. But the methods currently in plan for Poland probably all are. True, they have very different distributional implications.

Some benefit more or less all: this is the case for mass privatization. Some are likely to benefit workers more than others: this is the case for liquidation, especially if the leasing terms are made more lenient. True also, they differ in the shadow price they put on employment: sectoral privatization gives some leeway to the state to trade price for job guarantees; there is little reason to expect investment funds in mass privatization or management companies to have such concerns. More importantly, however, these approaches all provide vehicles to do what we argued earlier may be crucial to achieve privatization, the rough cutting up of firms before privatization. Mass privatization delegates this job and the incentives to carry it out to the investment funds. Sectoral privatization gives the job to the state. Privatization through restructuring gives the job and very strong incentives to the restructurers themselves. The problems we identified earlier in liquidation, the difficulty of starting the process when some activities must close as a result of privatization, may be fading as a result of the evolution of state firms themselves: when firms are facing almost certain collapse, workers and managers are more open to any solution in which at least some jobs can be saved.

Approving these methods in general is not the same as approving them in detail. We take up one issue here because it is of general relevance and extreme importance. It is clear that the transformation of state firms, if it is to happen, will require substantial foreign investment and expertise. The attitude of Poland to this point has been ambiguous, reflecting domestic political worries. One way to alleviate antiforeign feelings is to make clear to the people that they will benefit from such investment. Mass privatization naturally provides such a way, by allowing people to see how the values of their shares increase when firms in the funds' portfolios are sold to foreigners. For this reason alone, allowing for trading of shares much earlier than currently planned is essential. But there are other reasons as well, as is clear from voucher privatization in Czechoslovakia: distribution and trading of shares creates a strong constituency for capitalism. Strong warnings by the state about thin markets at the beginning and the likelihood of price increases in the future are probably enough to avoid the Czechoslovak excesses.

Cleaning Up Banks' Balance Sheets

When state firms are restructured, they will have to invest in new equipment. So will new private firms if they are to reach larger size and better efficiency; as we saw earlier, they are using old capital and need to modernize as well. Creating efficient financial intermediation, getting foreign capital, raises many issues. We shall take just one, which is urgent, the cleanup of banks' balance sheets, especially those of the large commercial banks.[28]

Thanks to the high inflation of 1989, the debt positions of state firms had been nearly wiped out as the reform program started. But, as we have seen, those debt positions have again steadily increased since then. As a result, banks' portfolios again include a significant proportion of nonperforming loans. Should anything be done about it?

One answer is that nothing should be done. The loans are not, for the most part, random legacies of the previous regime, but rather the result of decisions of banks and firms since reform started. Banks should therefore provision those loans, and write them off. But this answer is, unfortunately, unacceptable. While the exact scope of the writeoffs is still unclear, it probably exceeds the provisions that banks can afford to make over a reasonable period of time, say a few years. And as long as the bad loans are not written down, the banking system will be subject to runs and financial instability. Thus, cleaning up the balance sheets of banks cannot be avoided.

The obvious issue involved in designing a cleanup of banks is the familiar one of time consistency and credibility. A cleanup amounts to partial forgiveness of past bad behavior: because it would be socially costly to let banks default, and because the bad debts affect the efficiency of new lending, the government makes up for those bad debts, in part or in total. But if one cleanup only increases the perceived probability of another one later, it will induce bad behavior again. Thus, ideally, one wants to associate cleanups with a specific event, an event that will not happen again. This could have been the start of reform: the opportunity is now long gone, and in the case of Poland most of the bad debt has accumulated since reform anyway. It could have been associated with the corporatization of banks; the opportunity has just passed, as commercial banks were corporatized in the fall of 1991. Waiting for the next obvious event, privatization of banks, implies waiting too long. The effects of anticipated debt forgiveness are obviously perverse, as it increases the incentives of firms and banks to engage in further bad behavior. Thus, cleaning up must be started now; even this will take some time. To avoid anticipation effects, it must be made clear that it will apply only to debts incurred before some recent, but past, date.

Cleaning up is then relatively straightforward. Loans must be examined. Those that cannot be repaid must be written off. Those that may be repaid, but only in part, must be written down. An alternative, which has been often suggested, is to transform some of those loans into equities. Those who suggest it often have in mind planting the seeds of a system of bank-firm relations in the German or Japanese mode. It is however unwise at this point to have banks have substantial equity positions. This will not solve the problem of bank liquidity; furthermore, the quality of such equity positions is likely to be bad, and to destabilize rather than stabilize the financial system. Once loans have been written down, and if the banks' own funds are not enough to provision those writeoffs and writedowns, the state must provide the difference, in the form for example of government bonds. Then, until privatization, supervision will be needed to avoid the risk of repeat bad loans to state firms. That such a cleanup operation may lead to a loss of credibility of the hard budget constraint, that the cleanup may be followed by some more of the same behavior, is a clear risk; there is however no alternative.

A plan along roughly these lines is currently being prepared in Poland. The estimates are that to reestablish reserves equal to 12.5 percent of loans, the state will need to issue and give bonds to banks in an amount equal to 2 percent of GDP. This is a small amount to reestablish a healthy commercial banking system. Once this is done, it will be easier for new borrowers to get loans, and to get them at lower rates.[29]

Protecting Those Affected by the Transformation

If privatization and transformation of state firms come about, and if investment increases, many jobs will disappear and many jobs will be created. It is difficult to predict with much confidence when job creation will overtake job destruction, and how much unemployment will further increase. The most recent numbers suggest that the worst may be over: for the first half of 1992, the decrease in employment in the state sector, about 100,000, was nearly exactly offset by an increase in private employment. But, we have argued, state sector employment needs to further decline substantially, and the private sector does not have the scope needed to pick up the slack. Under those conditions, the state must make sure that those who lose their jobs do not suffer unduly. This raises another large set of issues, about labor mobility, the housing market and housing privatization, unemployment benefits, and so on. We again briefly take up only one issue here, that of unemployment benefits, which, we suspect, will soon become a central political issue.

One lesson from high unemployment in Western Europe has been that persistently high unemployment leads to the emergence of a "culture of unemployment," with many of the unemployed becoming disenfranchised. This lesson has led to a redesign of unemployment benefit systems, with decreasing benefits after a while, so as to induce the unemployed to take a job rather than become long term unemployed. This lesson has also been read by Eastern European countries which have put or are about to put limits on the length of unemployment benefits. Given the situation of these countries, and the many uncertainties about the rate of job creation, this may however turn out to be a bad idea, socially and politically. Forcing the long-term unemployed to find a job makes sense when new jobs are available. At this point in Poland, the monthly exit rate of the unemployment register is equal to 2 percent, a small fraction of what it is in Western countries; in many of the smaller cities, and even more so in the countryside, there are truly no jobs to be found. At the same time, a large number of unemployed have already or are soon going to have been unemployed for more than a year, thus becoming ineligible for unemployment benefits. It is not clear what purpose is served in this context by limiting the length of unemployment benefits—apart obviously from reducing state expenditures. The presence of a large number of unemployed without benefits may put some pressure on the wage. But the social cost may be considerable, and of all the factors limiting growth of new jobs, wages are not the most important. Even given the tight budget situation, the state can afford the cost of longer unemployment benefits. Many abuses can be prevented by the right design, such as, for example, making those benefits contingent on the unemployment rate of the city or the region, tying it to workfare programs, and the like. More generally, the temptations that Poland resisted earlier this year are likely to come again, in Poland and elsewhere. The constituency for reform must be nurtured by the government.[30] Thus, the strategy of reform must be not only to foster growth and job creation but also to take some care of those who lose in the process.

Statistical Appendix
on Russia

Monthly Inflation

	CPI (Dec. 1990 = 100)	WPI (Dec. 1990 = 100)	% change, CPI	% change, WPI
Feb. 92	1243	3750	38	75
Mar. 92	1613	4804	30	28
Apr. 92	1962	5621	22	17
May 92	2197	6914	12	23
Jun. 92	2606	9403	19	36
Jul. 92	2893	11000	11	17
Aug. 92	3153	12430	9	13
Sep. 92	3531	14171	12	14
Oct. 92	4344	17997	23	27
Nov. 92	5473	22856	26	27
Dec. 92	6841	27427	25	20
Jan. 93	8688	36203	27	32

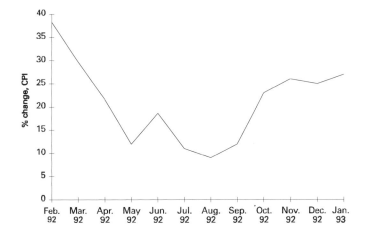

Weekly Inflation

Week ending	CPI (% change)	Food (% change)	Nonfood (% change)
29 Sep. 92	5.9	5.1	6.9
6 Oct. 92	6.6	7.1	6.0
13 Oct. 92	4.8	4.7	4.9
20 Oct. 92	4.7	5.6	3.4
27 Oct. 92	5.2	6.1	4.1
3 Nov. 92	5.8	6.6	4.8
10 Nov. 92	5.0	6.4	3.0
17 Nov. 92	4.0	3.8	4.4
24 Nov. 92	4.8	6.0	3.2
1 Dec. 92	6.7	7.9	5.1
8 Dec. 92	4.5	4.7	4.4
15 Dec. 92	4.6	4.7	4.5
22 Dec. 92	5.9	7.2	4.3
29 Dec. 92	7.4	10.0	3.9
5 Jan. 93	8.8	12.1	4.3
12 Jan. 93	4.1	4.2	3.9
19 Jan. 93	6.3	7.6	4.5
26 Jan. 93	3.6	2.1	5.6
2 Feb. 93	6.0	7.1	4.6
9 Feb. 93	5.6	4.5	7.1
16 Feb. 93	4.6	4.3	4.9

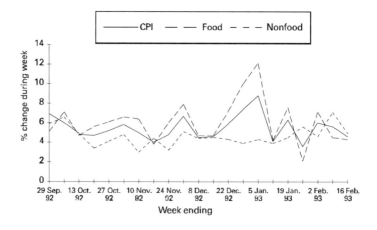

Monetary and Credit Aggregates

	Rubles (billion)			% growth during month		
	Total CBR credit[1]	Currency[2]	M2[3]	Total CBR credit	Currency	M2
Feb. 92	325	216	1204	39	13	12
Mar. 92	485	255	1369	49	18	14
Apr. 92	687	321	1506	42	26	10
May 92	833	369	1641	21	15	9
Jun. 92	1359	458	2093	63	24	28
Jul. 92	2009	645	2668	48	41	27
Aug. 92	3116	830	3422	55	29	28
Sep. 92	3866	998	4515	24	20	32
Oct. 92	4101	1196	5722	6	20	27
Nov. 92	4507	1449	6038	10	21	6
Dec. 92	6294	1716	7114	40	18	18
Jan. 93		1940			13	

1. Total CBR credit equals Central Bank of Russia credit to commercial banks plus CBR credit to other CIS republics plus CBR credit to the government plus CBR credit to enterprises.
2. All currency in circulation, including currency held by enterprises.
3. M2 indicates currency in circulation, demand deposits, and time deposits.

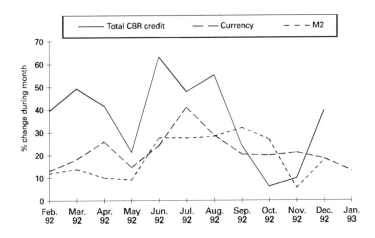

Wages and Incomes

	Average wage (rubles/ month)	Income of the population (billion rubles/ month)	Real per capita income (Jan. 1991 = 100)[1]	Wage growth (% monthly)	Income growth (% monthly)	Real per capita income growth (% monthly)
Feb. 92	2004	174	44	39	46	6
Mar. 92	2726	226	44	36	39	0
Apr. 92	3024	276	44	11	22	0
May 92	3672	274	39	21	0	−11
Jun. 92	5067	369	45	38	35	13
Jul. 92	5452	511	56	8	38	25
Aug. 92	5870	538	54	8	5	−4
Sep. 92	7379	624	55	26	16	3
Oct. 92	8853	758	55	20	21	−1
Nov. 92	10576	907	52	19	20	−5
Dec. 92	16071	1466	69	52	62	32
Jan. 93		1179	43		−20	−38

1. Per capita income per month deflated by the CPI.

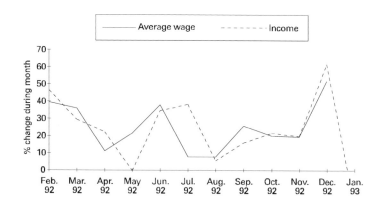

Velocity of Circulation for Purchasing Consumer Goods and Services[1]

	Consumer expenditure (billion rubles)	Currency velocity	M2 velocity
1992 Q1	358	0.59	0.10
1992 Q2	587	0.57	0.12
Jul. 92	259	0.48	0.11
Aug. 92	305	0.42	0.10
Sep. 92	386	0.42	0.10
Oct. 92	469	0.43	0.09
Nov. 92	558	0.42	0.10
Dec. 92	851	0.54	0.13
Jan. 93	799	0.44	

1. Velocity of circulation for purchasing consumer goods and services is defined as consumers' expenditure divided by the relevant monetary aggregate obtaining at the midpoint of the given period (assuming a constant growth rate over the appropriate month). The Q1 and Q2 velocity figures are given on a monthly basis in order to facilitate comparisons with the more recent monthly figures.

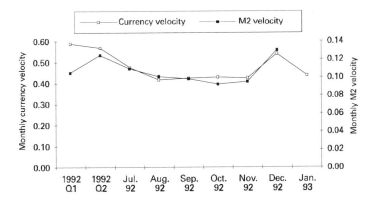

Velocity of Circulation for Purchasing GDP[1]

	GDP (billion rubles)	Currency velocity	M2 velocity
Feb. 92	481	2.36	0.42
Mar. 92	558	2.38	0.43
Apr. 92	645	2.25	0.45
May 92	739	2.15	0.47
Jun. 92	958	2.33	0.52
Jul. 92	1122	2.06	0.47
Aug. 92	1238	1.69	0.41
Sep. 92	1406	1.54	0.36
Oct. 92	1772	1.62	0.35
Nov. 92	2182	1.66	0.37
Dec. 92	2584	1.64	0.39
Jan. 93	3200	1.75	

1. Velocity of circulation for purchasing GDP is defined as gross domestic product divided by the relevant monetary aggregate obtaining at the mid-point of the given month (calculated assuming a constant growth rate over the month).

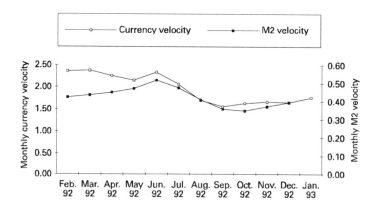

Nominal Exchange Rate (rubles/$US)

	Noncash[1]	Cash
14 Jan.	180	137
18 Feb.	170	112
17 Mar.	161	115
14 Apr.	155	125
14 May	128	124
16 Jun.	119	125
16 Jul.	136	143
18 Aug.	163	181
22 Sep.	241	221
8 Oct.	334	295
20 Oct.	368	318
10 Nov.	403	409
24 Nov.	450	453
1 Dec.	417	474
3 Dec.	398	
8 Dec.	419	440
10 Dec.	419	
15 Dec.	418	
17 Dec.	416	
22 Dec.	415	469
24 Dec.	415	
5 Jan.	417	
12 Jan.	423	475
14 Jan.	442	
19 Jan.	475	500
21 Jan.	493	
26 Jan.	568	550
28 Jan.	572	
2 Feb.	572	663
4 Feb.	572	
9 Feb.	561	660
11 Feb.	560	
16 Feb.	559	640
18 Feb.	559	
23 Feb.	576	

1. The noncash rate represents the price of the dollar on the Moscow Interbank Currency Exchange.

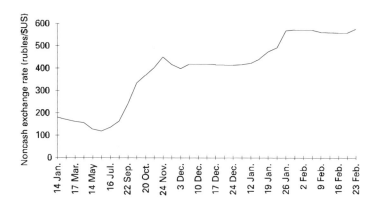

Real Exchange Rate[1] (rubles/$US) (US price level)/(Russian price level)

Mid-month	Noncash exchange rate	CPI (midmonth)[2] (Dec. 1990 = 100)	US CPI (Dec. 1990 = 100)	Real exchange rate (Apr. 1991 = 100)
Apr. 91	30	151	101	100
Jan. 92	180	484	102	247
Feb. 92	170	1057	103	107
Mar. 92	151	1416	103	76
Apr. 92	155	1779	103	58
May 92	128	2076	104	41
Jun. 92	119	2393	104	33
Jul. 92	136	2746	104	33
Aug. 92	163	3020	104	36
Sep. 92	204	3337	105	42
Oct. 92	338	3916	105	59
Nov. 92	419	4876	105	59
Dec. 92	418	6119	105	47
Jan. 93	442	7710	106	39
Feb. 93	559	9714	106	40

1. The real exchange rate is defined as the nominal exchange rate (rubles/$US) multiplied by the ratio of the US price level to the Russian price level.
2. The Russian midmonth CPI is calculated assuming a constant inflation rate over the month.
3. The February figure assumes a Russian inflation rate of 25% monthly and a US inflation rate of 0.2% monthly.

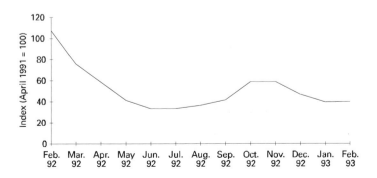

Wages and Pensions

	Average wage	Minimum pension	Minimum wage	Real wage[1] index (1990 = 100)	Minimum pension/ average wage
1985	201	50	70	75	0.25
1990	297	70	70	100	0.24
1991 Q1	315	80	70	90	0.25
Q2	429	165	130	70	0.38
Q3	551	165	130	87	0.30
Q4	770	234	192	105	0.30
Jan. 92	1438	342	342	51	0.24
Feb. 92	2004	542	342	52	0.27
Mar. 92	2726	542	342	54	0.20
Apr. 92	3024	642	342	50	0.21
May 92	3672	900	900	54	0.25
Jun. 92	5067	900	900	63	0.18
Jul. 92	5452	900	900	61	0.17
Aug. 92	5870	900	900	60	0.15
Sep. 92	7379	1350	900	67	0.18
Oct. 92	8853	1350	900	66	0.15
Nov. 92	10576	2250	900	62	0.21
Dec. 92	16071	2250	900	76	0.14
Jan. 93		2250			

1. The real wage is defined as the average nominal wage deflated by the CPI.

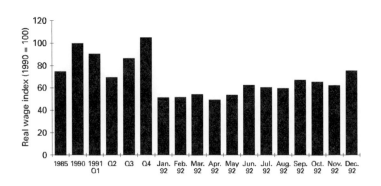

Real Consumer Expenditure

	Consumer expenditure (billion rubles)	CPI (Dec. 1990 = 100)	Real consumer expenditure (billion rubles)[1]
1991 Q1	82	112	73
Q2	106	198	54
Q3	133	204	65
Q4	189	235	80
1992 Q1	358	1252	29
Q2	587	2255	26
Q3	949	3214	30
Q4	1878	5617	33
Jan. 93[2]	2396	8688	28

1. December 1990 prices.
2. January 1993 on a quarterly basis.

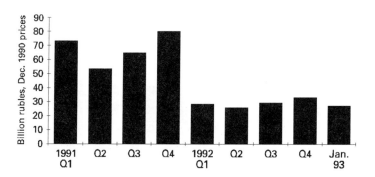

Industrial Production

	Industrial production	Real % change (on year ago)	As % of year ago (real)	Index of real industrial production[1] (Dec. 1991 = 100)
Q1	1994	−13	87	98
Q2[2]	2941	−14	86	94
Jul. 92	1065	−22	79	83
Aug. 92	1369	−27	73	72
Sep. 92	1433	−25	75	80
Oct. 92	2098	−25	75	81
Nov. 92	2346	−24	76	79
Dec. 92	2889	−20	80	80
Jan. 93	2987	−20	80	75

1. Seasonally adjusted with weights from monthly production, 1989–1991. The raw (non–seasonally adjusted) data reflect the 1988 industrial price structure.
2. The quarterly figures are given on a monthly basis, calculated as the simple average of the constituent months.

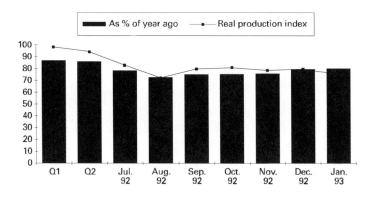

Unemployment and Vacancies (thousands of people)

	"Out of employ-ment"	Registered unemployed	Receiving benefits	In retraining	In public works	Vacancies
Jan. 92	485	69	18	4	1	586
Feb. 92	554	93	33	5	2	490
Mar. 92	616	118	53	7	4	451
Apr. 92	696	151	74	8	5	408
May 92	743	177	89	8	7	400
Jun. 92	779	203	108	8	13	399
Jul. 92	843	248	140	7	14	377
Aug. 92	888	303	173	7	15	364
Sep. 92	921	367	219	10	13	345
Oct. 92	982	442	267	14	8	316
Nov. 92	1011	518	317	20	6	295
Dec. 92	982	578	371	18	6	307
Jan. 93	1029	628	411	20	4	301

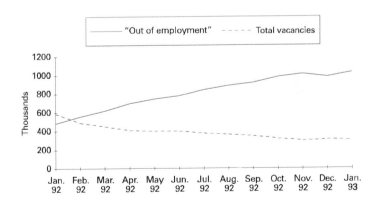

Privatization

	Number of firms privatized	Revenues from privatization (billion rubles)
Mar. 92	1352	2
Apr. 92	2995	3
May 92	5855	4
Jun. 92	8933	8
Jul. 92	12015	10
Aug. 92	17230	14
Sep. 92	22572	21
Oct. 92	29235	39
Nov. 92	34932	77
Dec. 92	46815	157

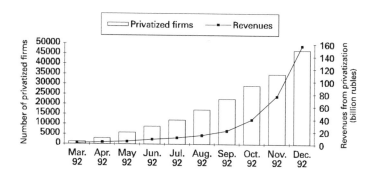

Notes

2 Stabilization versus Reform? Russia's First Year

1. A reasonable assumption in Russia is that the change in inflation is related to both the level of unemployment and the change in unemployment.

2. See also the articles by Russian ministers and Western advisers in Aslund and Layard (1993), and the Survey in the *Economist*, 5 December 1992.

3. There is little evidence that monopoly power was a major factor in the price overshoot (*Russian Economic Trends*, vol 1., no. 2, p. 29). Inflationary expectations seem a better explanation.

4. Up to July the government paid only half the market price for the compulsory sales of 40 percent of export earnings by raw material exporters. Since July the government has paid the full price, but the export tax has been raised to compensate for this extra cost. This is a much less important change than the requirement in July that 50 percent of *all* export earnings must be sold (30 percent to the government and 20 percent to the market).

5. During the year to November 1992, industrial production in Russia fell 23 percent and employment 4.5 percent.

6. The G7 debt negotiations in November 1991 were the first negotiations undertaken by the new government. Unfortunately they failed to take into account realities that were better perceived by the Russians. The negotiated deal led directly to the disastrous freezing of accounts by the Vnesheconom Bank. These negotiations set the precedent for somewhat arm's-length relationships.

7. Repayment by enterprises could be specified in dollars or in rubles at the prevailing exchange rate (since many enterprises will not be confident that convertibility will be maintained).

8. World Bank loans in these fields have already had good effects; see for example the Report of the Commission on Professional Preparation for the Market Economy (1992).

3 The Politics of Russian Privatization

This paper borrows from an earlier paper by Andrei Shleifer and Robert Vishny, "Privatization in Russia: First Steps" (NBER Conference on Reform in Eastern Europe, February 1992). The authors have benefited from working together with Jonathan Hay and Dmitri Vasiliev of GKI. Andrei Shleifer is grateful to the Bradley Foundation for financial support of this research.

4 Payments Arrangements among the Republics

1. There might be a need to use more frequent clearing in a case of hyperinflation so as to avoid a country buying early in the month and selling late. That is an important though still minor technical issue.

2. I owe the analogy to Michael Mussa.

3. James Boughton of the IMF estimates that an equivalent funding today would require $US 1.8 billion.

5 The Progress of Restructuring in Poland

The authors thank Jay Adams, Philippe Aghion, Brian Pinto, Michael Bruno, Stanislaw Gomulka, Stefan Kawalec, Janusz Lewandowski, Kevin McDonald, Mark Schaffer, and Jerzy Thieme for useful discussions and comments. They have also benefited from joint work with Andrew Berg.

1. Credibility is never acquired permanently. One of the themes of this chapter will be that credibility has since ebbed back and forth.

2. Many analyses of the Polish reform program and its macroeconomic effects are available. See in particular Lipton and Sachs (1990), Gomulka (1991), Berg and Sachs (1992), Dabrowski (1991a), Calvo and Coricelli (1991), Berg and Blanchard (1992), and Schaffer (1992b).

3. Because many prices had been liberalized earlier, price liberalization was not as drastic as is sometimes perceived. In particular, most food prices had been liberalized in August 1989. Price liberalization in January 1990 increased the proportion of free prices from 70–75 percent to about 90 percent.

4. For a description of the methods of privatization, and an analysis of how well they have worked, see Berg (1992). For a recent discussion of privatization, see also Dabrowski (1991b).

5. But only four ministers, Krysztof Lis, Waldemar Kuczynski, Janusz Lewandowski, Tomasz Gruszecki, and again Janusz Lewandowski.

6. Hungary for example has gone back and forth between care and speed. Spontaneous privatization was an example of simple and low valuation leading to speedy privatization, but also to a political backlash triggered by its distributional implications. It was followed by more care, but a near stop in the speed of privatization.

7. In particular, the fact that some of these firms were energy-intensive and would do worse when energy prices were increased,

and that some others were highly dependent on CMEA trade, was not fully taken into account.

8. Lawrence Summers has suggested the following analogy from the real estate market. The advice to sellers in that market is that it is a bad idea when selling a house to radically redo the bathroom; the buyer is likely to have different preferences. But it is a good thing to give the house a coat of paint, and to clear up any issues about legal title.

9. Characterizations of the evolution of state firms in 1990 and 1991, using sectoral and individual firm data, are given in Dabrowski, Federowicz, and Levitas (1991), Schaffer (1992c), and Berg and Blanchard (1992). McDonald and Sachs (1992) give a characterization of the weaknesses of state firms, as well as a number of specific examples.

10. The existence of these councils played an important role in shaping attitudes, however. Many of those now involved in re-form, and many of the new managers, gained experience from participating in workers' councils. Councils also played an impor-tant role in preventing attempts at recentralization.

11. The effects were sometimes positive, sometimes negative. While some managers were dismissed for being "socialist manag-ers," unprepared for a market economy, others were dismissed when they tried to restrict wage growth or restructure. See Dabrowski, Federowicz, and Levitas (1991).

12. This was discussed in our previous report. There are three caveats to be made here. The first is that this statement applies only when workers do not lose ownership when they leave the firm, either through layoffs or by quitting, thus only when own-ership titles are transferable; this was not the case in Yugoslavia, and is not the case in the transition. The second is that, if capital markets are imperfect—as they are likely to be—workers may put too much weight on current revenues, leading firms to act with too short a horizon. The third is that in the presence of nonworker minority shareholders, there is a strong incentive for workers to

distribute revenues through wages rather than profits. This can be resolved either by restrictions on the voting rights of workers, or by specific covenants protecting the right of minority shareholders.

13. Some of the privatization mechanisms actually have perverse incentive effects, as insiders—managers and workers—can decrease the selling price by mismanaging their firms. This is, however, a dangerous game to play. And it does not appear to have been played.

14. This statistic is partly misleading, however, as firms have financial incentives to report group layoffs as voluntary separations. Anecdotal evidence suggests that they have indeed often done so.

15. The reasons why are analyzed in Berg and Blanchard (1992). For fluctuations in the attitudes of firms vis-à-vis the *popiwek,* see Dabrowski (1991a).

16. Not all the decrease comes from the transfer to wages. Part of it also comes from the interaction between inflation, the absence of inflation accounting, and the tax system. See Schaffer (1992c, 1992a).

17. Such a scenario can actually be observed in East Germany.

18. See for example Jorgensen et al. (1991).

19. Food processing, the only 2-digit sector that grew in Poland in 1991, had been characterized in earlier studies as one of the sectors with the largest negative value added at world prices, thus as one of the sectors with the least hope of surviving price liberalization. The same lack of correlation between predicted and actual declines has been documented by Borensztein, Demekas, and Ostry (1992) for Czechoslovakia, Bulgaria, and Romania.

20. These numbers do not include cooperatives. Cooperatives were initially counted in official data as being in the state sector. They are now counted as part of the private sector. The share of private and cooperative employment in total nonagricultural employment went from 31 percent in 1989 to 38 percent in 1991.

21. It is often said that there are nearly no data on the private sector in Poland. This is not quite true, and the official statistics probably capture fairly accurately businesses when they reach a certain size, often 5 or more employees. For a number of purposes, these are the firms one is most interested in. There are also now a number of surveys on the behavior of private firms: three useful ones are by Johnson (1991), Webster (1992), and by Pinto, Bella, and Krajewski (1992).

22. This is another case where the current experience in Russia, and the use of bank credit to keep firms afloat, comes to mind.

23. This argument has been made in the context of reform by Perotti (1992).

24. This number is slightly misleading, as a high proportion of those arrears is accounted for by one large firm.

25. Banaszuk (1992) gives a useful description of bankruptcy proceedings, as well as a number of case studies.

26. For a discussion of how to design a good bankruptcy law, see Aghion, Hart, and Moore (1992).

27. The idea underlying this approach can be traced to a proposal by Milton Friedman in *Newsweek* in 1976. An elaboration of this plan was developed by Lipton and Sachs (1991). Our own, closely related proposal was presented by Blanchard et al. (1991).

28. Other banks are in trouble. The Bank for Housing is in a situation not unlike the American S&L's at the time of deregulation. For assets it has loans made at very low rates, but now pays more for its liabilities. The issue for the state is one of income distribution, of whether to increase the rates on loans or to subsidize the low rates.
For a discussion of the same issues in the Hungarian context, see Estrin, Hare, and Suranyi (1992). See also Begg and Portes (1992).

29. The spreads may not decrease very much, however. An often heard argument is that the desire to provision bad loans has led banks to charge large spreads of lending over borrowing rates. The

argument is equivalent to saying that firms that want more profits will simply increase prices, and seems equally fallacious. The average spreads primarily reflect monopoly power, and thus may not decrease much after a bank cleanup.

30. For an interesting analysis of how to keep consensus in favor of reform, see Freeman (1992).

References

Aghion, P., J. Fleming, and J. Pisany-Ferry. 1991. "A Framework for a Multilateral Clearing Scheme." Mimeo, The European Bank, London.

Aghion, P., O. Hart, and J. Moore. 1992. "The Economics of Bankruptcy Reform, 1." Mimeo, Cambridge University.

Aslund, A. 1991. "Prospects for a Successful Change of Economic System in Russia." Mimeo, Stockholm, October.

Aslund, A., and R. Layard, eds. 1993. *Changing the Economic System in Russia*. London: Pinter Publishers.

Banaszuk, Mariusz. 1992. "Polish Bankruptcy Law in (In)action." Mimeo, Sachs and Associates, Warsaw.

Begg, D., and R. Portes. 1992. "Enterprise Debt and Economic Transformation: Financial Restructuring of the State Sector in Central and Eastern Europe." Working paper, Center for Economic Policy Research, London.

Berg, A. 1992. "The Logistics of Privatization: The Case of Poland." Mimeo, presented at NBER Conference on the Transition in Eastern Europe.

Berg, A., and O. Blanchard. 1992. "Stabilization and Transition: Poland 1990–1991." Mimeo, presented at NBER Conference on the Transition in Eastern Europe.

Berg, A., and J. Sachs. 1992. "Trade Reform and Adjustment in Eastern Europe: The Case of Poland." *Economic Policy.*

Blanchard, O., R. Dornbusch, P. Krugman, R. Layard, and L. Summers. 1991. *Reform in Eastern Europe.* Cambridge: MIT Press.

Bofinger, P. 1990. "A Multilateral Payments Union for Eastern Europe?" Discussion Paper no. 458. Center for Economic Policy Research, London.

Bofinger, P. 1991a. "Options for the Payments and Exchange Rate System in Eastern Europe." *European Economy* (Special Issue: The Path to Reform in Central and Eastern Europe), no. 2, 243–262.

Bofinger, P. 1991b. "The Difficult Path to Convertibility in the Soviet Union." Mimeo, Landeszentralbank Baden-Württemberg.

Borensztein, E., D. Demekas, and J. Ostry. 1992. "The Output Decline in the Aftermath of Reform: The Cases of Bulgaria, Czechoslovakia and Romania." International Monetary Fund Working Paper no. 92-59.

Bruno, M. 1992. "Stabilization and Reform in Eastern Europe: A Preliminary Evaluation." Mimeo, International Monetary Fund, Washington, January.

Calvo, G., and F. Coricelli. 1991. "Stagflationary Effects of Stabilization Programs in Reforming Socialist Countries: Supply Side Versus Demand Side Factors." Mimeo, International Monetary Fund, Washington.

Collignon, S. 1991. "A Proposal to Create an ECU Zone to Assist Eastern Europe's Transition to a Market Economy." Mimeo, Association for the Monetary Union of Europe, Paris.

Collins, S., and D. Rodrik. 1991. *Eastern Europe and the Soviet Union in the World Economy.* Policy Analysis in International Economics no. 32. Washington: Institute for International Economics.

Dabrowski, J., M. Federowicz, and A. Levitas. 1991. "Polish State Enterprises and the Properties of Performance: Stabilization, Marketization, Privatization." *Politics and Society* 19, no. 4, 403–437.

Dabrowski, M. 1991a. "The Polish Stabilization 1990–1991." *Journal of International and Comparative Economics* 1, no. 4 (1992), 295–324.

Dabrowski, M. 1991b. "Privatization in Poland." *Communist Economies and Economic Transformation* 3, no. 3, 317–326.

De Long, B., and B. Eichengreen. 1993. "The Marshall Plan: History's Most Successful Structural Adjustment Program." In R. Dornbusch, W. Nölling, and R. Layard, eds., *Postwar Economic Reconstruction and Lessons for the East Today.* Cambridge: MIT Press.

Ellman, M. 1992. "Shock Therapy in Russia: Failure or Partial Success?" RFE/RL Research Report, vol. 1, no. 34 (August).

Ellman, M., and R. Layard. 1993. "Prices, Incomes and Hardship." In Aslund and Layard 1993.

Estrin, S., P. Hare, and M. Suranyi. 1992. "Banking in Transition: Development and Current Problems in Hungary." Discussion Paper no. 68. Center for Economic Performance, London School of Economics.

Freeman, R. 1992. "What Direction for Labor Market Institutions in Eastern and Central Europe?" Mimeo, presented at NBER Conference on the Transition in Eastern Europe.

Gomulka, S. 1991. "The Causes of Recession Following Stabilization." *Comparative Economic Studies* 32, no. 2, 71–89.

Greene, J., and P. Isard. 1991. *Currency Convertibility and the Transformation of Centrally Planned Economies.* IMF Occasional Paper no. 81. Washington: International Monetary Fund.

Gros, D. 1991. "A Soviet Payments Union?" Mimeo, Center for European Policy Studies, Brussels.

Gros, D., J. Pisany-Ferry, and A. Sapir. 1992. "Inter-State Economic Relations in the Former Soviet Union." Mimeo, Center for European Policy Studies, Brussels.

Grossman, Sanford J., and Oliver D. Hart. 1986. "The Costs and Benefits of Ownership: A Theory of Vertical and Lateral Integration." *Journal of Political Economy* 94 (August), 691–719.

Hamilton, C., and A. Winters. 1992. "Opening Up International Trade with Eastern Europe." *Economic Policy* (April).

Havrylyshyn, O., and J. Williamson. 1991. *From Soviet DisUnion to Eastern Economic Community?* Policy Analysis in International Economics no. 35. Washington: Institute for International Economics.

Hussain, A., and N. Stern. 1991. "Economic Reform in China." *Economic Policy* (April).

International Monetary Fund. 1992 *Common Issues and Interrepublic Relations in the Former USSR.* Washington: International Monetary Fund.

International Monetary Fund et al. 1991. *A Study of the Soviet Economy.* Washington: International Monetary Fund.

Johnson, S. 1991. "Private Business in Eastern Europe." Mimeo, Duke University, December.

Jorgensen, E., A. Gelb, and I. Singh. 1991. "Life after the Polish 'Big Bang': Representative Episodes of Enterprise Behavior." In Vittorio Corbo, Fabrizio Coricelli, and Jan Bossak, eds., *Reforming Central and Eastern European Economies: Initial Results and Challenges.* Washington: World Bank (mimeo).

Kaplan, J., and G. Schleiminger. 1989. *The European Payments Union.* Oxford: Oxford University Press.

Kenen, P. 1991. "Transitional Arrangements for Trade and Payments among the CMEA Countries." *IMF Staff Papers* 38, no. 2.

Lipton, D., and J. Sachs. 1990. "Creating a Market Economy in Eastern Europe: The Case of Poland." *Brookings Papers on Economic Activity* no. 1, 75–133.

Lipton, D., and J. Sachs. 1991. "Privatization in Eastern Europe: The Case of Poland." *Brookings Papers on Economic Activity.*

Lipton, D., and J. Sachs. 1992. "Prospects for Russia's Economic Reform." *Brookings Papers on Economic Activity.*

McDonald, K., and J. Sachs. 1992. "Transformation of the Polish Economy at the Enterprise Level." Mimeo, Cambridge, Mass., June.

Michalopoulos, C., and D. Tarr. 1992. *Trade and Payments Arrangements for States of the Former USSR.* Washington: World Bank.

Milward, A. 1987. *The Reconstruction of Western Europe 1945–51.* Berkeley: University of California Press.

Patterson, G. 1953. *Survey of the United States International Finance 1952.* Princeton: Princeton University Press.

Perotti, E. 1992. "Bank Lending in Transition Economies." Mimeo, Boston University and London School of Economics.

Petrakov, N., et al. 1992. "Pravitel'stvo utratilo kontrol' nad ekonomicheskimi protsessami." *Nezavisimaya gazeta* (6 March), 4.

Pinto, B., M. Bella, and S. Krajewski. 1992. "Microeconomics of Transformation in Poland: A Survey of State Enterprise Responses." Mimeo, World Bank, June.

Russian Economic Trends. Published for the government of the Russian Federation by Whurr Publishers Ltd., London.

Sachs, J. 1991. "The Economic Transformation of Eastern Europe: The Case of Poland." Frank E. Seidman Distinguished Award in Political Economy, Rhodes College, Memphis.

Schaffer, M. 1992a. "The Enterprise Sector and Emergence of the Polish Fiscal Crisis 1990–91." Mimeo, Center for Economic Performance, London School of Economics.

Schaffer, M. 1992b. "Poland." In David Dyker, ed., *The European Economy.* White Plains, N.Y.: Longman.

Schaffer, M. 1992c. "The Polish State-Owned Enterprise Sector and the Recession in 1990." *Comparative Economic Studies.*

Soros, G. 1991. "An Interrepublican Payments System." Mimeo, The Soros Foundation, New York.

Tirole, Jean. 1991. "Privatization in Eastern Europe: Incentives and the Economics of Transition." In Olivier Jean Blanchard and Stanley Fischer, eds., *NBER Macroeconomics Annual.* Cambridge: MIT Press.

Van Brabant, J. 1991. "Key Problems in Creating a Central European Payments Union." Banca Nazionale del Lavoro *Quarterly Review,* no. 177 (June), 119–150.

Webster, L. 1992. "Survey of Private Firms in Poland." Mimeo, World Bank, Washington.

Williamson, J. 1991. *Currency Convertibility in Eastern Europe.* Washington: Institute for International Economics.

Winiecki, J. 1990. "Post-Soviet Type Economies in Transition: What Have We Learned from the Polish Transition Programme in Its First Year?" *Weltwirtschaftliches Archiv* 126, no. 4, 781–783.

World Bank. 1992. *Russian Economic Reform: Crossing the Threshold of Structural Change.* Vol. I: Main Report.

Yavlinsky, G. 1992. "Reforms in Russia in Spring 1992." *Moscow News,* nos. 21 and 22.

Yeager, L. 1966. *International Monetary Relations.* New York: Harper and Row.

Index